JASON PERRY

OF **PLUS ONE**

WITH **Steve Keels**

YOU ARE
NOT
YOUR
OWN

living for God

B&H
BROADMAN
&HOLMAN
PUBLISHERS

Nashville, Tennessee

0-8054-2591-8

Published by Broadman & Holman Publishers,
Nashville, Tennessee

Subject Heading: YOUTH/CHRISTIAN LIVING

3 4 5 6 7 8 9 10 06 05 04 03 02

To Pastor Tim Johnson:

It was because of you that this book was even possible. You've changed my life, and I am forever grateful. You are truly my hero and the kind of man I want to become. This is the beginning of an amazing journey serving the King together, and I can't wait.

Contents

Foreword

Mr. McPherson always wore his kilt to church on Sunday. He was a striking, imposing figure, one of many guests gathered for lunch in the house of a friend. The young man of the house, a teenager, was on the fringe of the mealtime conversation until, quite out of the blue, McPherson asked him, "An' whit aboot you, son? Whit are ye gonae mak' o' yersel?" I can still recall the embarrassment of the young man as he scrambled for some kind of sensible, acceptable answer. After all, how many teenagers have figured out what they are doing later that day, much less with the rest of their lives?

While it may not be true to say that questions about identity and meaning *plague* teenagers, they do *confront* those questions: *Who am I? Where did I come from? Where am I going? And why?* If they fail to provide themselves with satisfying answers to the basic questions of life, they are liable to cast around in many directions to make sense of it all.

It would be good if we could report that the Church is doing a terrific job of meeting this generation on their turf and seeing them converted by the power of truth. Though there are encouraging exceptions, in far too many cases there is a significant credibility gap caused by those whose Christianity is marked by an operational efficiency, not a life-changing walk with Christ.

As a father and pastor, I am constantly on the lookout for good material for the teenage and college population. I am familiar with and thankful for the books that fall in the category of "fatherly advice," but there is a dearth of helpful writing coming from the pens of the MTV generation.

For this reason I was delighted to discover Jason Perry's book, which charges into that void. He has written with an honesty that his peers will find refreshingly helpful. They are fed up with their parents' feeble attempts at being straightforward (when in fact we parents are merely beating around the bush). In tackling issues of peer pressure, he acknowledges that relationships are seldom neutral. After all, there are people in whose company it is easy to be good, and others in whose company it is easy to be bad.

As Jason says, "Friendships are important because they often hold the power of spiritual life or spiritual death." From his own experience, he helps the reader recognize the folly and futility of life "on the fence" and wrestles with the implications of Jesus' prayer that His children would not be removed from the world but be kept from the evil one.

Jason acknowledges the challenges of having the boat in the water without the water being in the boat.

At the heart of the book is a wonderful chapter on the vital importance of the Word of God as food for the journey, light for the path, and renewal for the mind. Vance Havner, the quick-witted Southern preacher, used to say, "Sin will keep you from this book or this book will keep you from sin." At a time when scant attention is paid to the Bible even in church services and the memorization of Scripture is a thing of the past, reading chapter 5 of Jason's book caused me to stand up and cheer in the privacy of my study.

Here is solid advice from an average nineteen-year-old guy who decided to take God's Word seriously and discovered that it purified his mind, stirred his heart, helped him to resist temptation, and increased his ability to give an answer to those who ask about how they can maintain a meaningful walk with God.

It has been vitally important for Jason to have someone alongside him as a coach and encourager. His experience illustrates the Scripture that reminds us that "two are better than one because they have a good return for their labor. For if either of them falls, the one will lift up his companion" (Ecclesiastes 4:9–10).

Whether the spiritual coach is a father, mother, friend, or pastor, each of us is helped by having someone to hold us accountable. By the time Paul writes his last letter to Timothy, the disappointments that Paul had known in the past concerning John Mark are behind him, and he asks that John Mark might visit him because "he is helpful to me in my ministry." John Mark's progress in the faith was under God largely due to the willingness of Barnabas to work with him even when Paul had grown impatient with him.

Jason seeks to encourage others with the encouragement he has received. He is keenly aware that you can never lead souls to heaven unless you're climbing yourself. You need not be very high up, but you must be climbing.

Throughout this book is a recurring emphasis on the fact that none of us lives to ourselves or dies to ourselves. Instead, we are encouraged to live in such a way that our lives may be a help and not a hindrance to others.

Finally, the book points to Christ and His Word. There is hope here for young people who feel that the mistakes already made disqualify them from any future usefulness. With God, failure need never be final. He is so wise and wonderful that even our mistakes and disappointments may become, by His grace, springboards for service. For as the title reminds us, "You are not your own, for you were bought at a price; therefore glorify God in your body" (1 Corinthians 6:19b–20). So read on to discover how to flee the passions of youth and become an example to your peers in speech, life, love, faith, and purity.

ALISTAIR BEGG
Parkside Church, Cleveland, Ohio

Acknowledgments

I would like to start by thanking the two men who made this vision come to pass: Steve Keels and Dan Vorm. Let's start by remembering how good it felt after we handed the manuscript in. Wow. We did it, and you guys made it happen. I can't thank you enough for the long nights and early mornings and for sacrificing family time and other responsibilities to make this project work. I sincerely thank you from the bottom of my heart. Steve, now we can talk about the Bible and theology all we want.

I'd like to thank the families of both Steve and Dan. I appreciate your being so flexible and giving. May God bless you.

There are so many people that have impacted my life, so I'd like to mention a few.

I would first like to thank my family. Thanks, Mom and Dad, for being obedient to the voice of God and letting me walk in my destiny at such a young age. Your support and love are felt wherever I go. Aaron, Curtis, and Christi—you guys are the best brothers and sister a person could have. You have always supported me in everything I've done, so thank you.

I would like to thank Gary Terashita, Stephanie Huffman, and everyone at Broadman & Holman for believing in me and putting faith in me to get the job done.

I would like to thank my management team (Mitch, Amy, and Teresa) and especially Brent Gibbs for all your hard work in making sure everything was taken care of. Brent, you're awesome. I'm looking forward to learning so much more.

Thanks to Richard Curtis and Lynn Morrow for making sure everything was done right.

Thanks so much to Alistair Begg for reading my book and offering such kind words to help guide all who read this.

I'd like to thank two very special people who will never know how much they impacted my life: Dr. and Mrs. Goida. Thank you for carrying out the work of the Lord.

I'd like to thank the people of Madison First Assembly. You have watched me grow up. And through it all, you have never stopped praying for me, supporting me, and loving me. Thank you. I love you.

I would like to thank all my pastors and spiritual family at Bethel World Outreach Center. You have changed my life and given me a message.

I would like to thank the rest of the Johnson family, particularly La'chelle. Other than my mother, you have impacted my life more than any woman I know. I have learned so much from you.

I would like to thank all the guys from Plus One: Jeremy, Nathan, Nate, and Gabe. First of all, thanks for letting me in the band two years ago. Thank you for all your love and encouragement and, most of all, your tolerance of my spending all my time working on this book. You guys are so patient and understanding. Thank you.

There are so many people to thank. If I forgot anyone, please forgive me.

May God richly bless you all.

A Date with Destiny

In the middle of Plus One's first tour with Jaci Velasquez, our schedule had brought us back to Nashville, and I found myself with a couple of free days before boarding the bus for our next concert. I was glad to have a break. Life on the road is great, but every once in awhile, it's nice to get off the stage and live a normal life.

This break in the schedule happened to fall right around Halloween. A friend told me about an event at a nearby church that evening, and since there wasn't much happening elsewhere, I decided to check it out. I had visited this church a couple of times during the previous summer, so I knew I'd run into some familiar faces. I wasn't expecting it to be a life-changing evening—it was just a chance to hang out, be cool, and see if I could meet some girls.

I nosed my 1987 Buick into a church parking space and began to walk toward the outdoor games and activities. As

CHAPTER ONE

I neared the main doors, I saw some people my age standing and talking. I walked up and introduced myself, enjoying the fact that several of them recognized me as Jason
from Plus One. One girl in particular caught my eye, and we
wandered off by ourselves and started talking. I thought to
myself, *Hey, this is going to be a great night after all. I'm glad
I came.* We chatted then headed into the gym to watch a
performance by the youth group.

As we found seats near the front, it became obvious that
the people around us recognized me. The performance
ended, and a man who appeared to be a pastor stood up in
front. With one ear, I was listening to him speak; I was most
concerned, however, with trying to impress those around me.

I'd grown up in a pastor's home, hearing sermon after
sermon. I sat there and thought to myself, *What does this guy
have to say that I don't already know?* But as this pastor spoke, I
realized there was something compelling about him. I was
drawn to his message—it felt like he was talking directly to
me. At the end of his talk, I sat down, acting cool and non-
chalant, waiting for the crowd to leave the room. Then I made
my way to the front where the pastor was talking with someone. After a few minutes, he turned his attention my way.

The pastor, whose name is Tim, is a big guy—about
twice my size. (Later on, I learned that he played in the NFL
for ten years—two years with the Pittsburgh Steelers, one
year with the Cincinnati Bengals, then seven years with the
Washington Redskins.) At first glance, it didn't appear that

we'd have much in common. He was an ex-pro athlete; I was a singer in a Christian boy band. Yet I felt somehow drawn to him. For some reason I knew that God wanted us to meet.

"Hey, that was really good," I said to the pastor, thinking that my affirmation would mean something to him. The pastor thanked me, then proceeded to ask me who I was and where I was from.

"My name is Jason Perry, and I'm a singer with a group called Plus One." I thought every Christian had heard of Plus One, but obviously he hadn't. In fact, he didn't seem impressed at all by my "celebrity" status. To him, it didn't seem to matter.

He introduced himself as Pastor Tim, one of the pastors on staff at the church. We started to talk, and before I knew it, we found ourselves conversing outside. Soon we were all alone in the parking lot—just us, a few scattered cars, and God.

As Pastor Tim and I talked about my life and my walk with God, it seemed as if this guy had known me a long time. I was amazed. My mouth hung open, and my eyes got as big as softballs. It was like he knew everything that was going on inside my head. For years I'd been wearing a mask. Not the kind that trick-or-treaters were wearing as they gathered candy in surrounding neighborhoods that Halloween night. No, my mask was one of religious pride, hiding all the sin that was in my heart—sin that was inwardly eating me alive.

Here was a stranger who was stripping away my spiritual mask as one might peel an onion. It didn't take long for Tim to figure out that I hadn't come to church that evening to hear from God. He knew I was there to hang out and project an image, and he called me on it. In all my years of growing up in church, I'd never had anyone get inside my life like he did that night. He didn't just assume that I was where I needed to be spiritually; he looked past the fact that I was a Christian singer and found the real Jason deep inside.

That evening, God knocked me off my high horse. I didn't see it coming, but now, looking back, I see how desperately I needed to be changed by the power of God. I was good at playing games with God. I could talk the talk as well as anybody. On the outside, I appeared to be the perfect Christian young man. On the inside, though, I was tired of leaving God on the fringes of my life.

Tim put his Bible up to my chest and challenged me to look up 2 Timothy 2:22. I promised to do so when I got home later that evening. We talked a little longer and then said good night. As I turned and walked to my car, my mind was in a fog. "What just happened to me?" I whispered to myself. I got in my car and started driving, unaware of anything except the unexpected conversation that had just taken place. As I drove toward my apartment, Tim's parting words burned themselves into my mind: "Son, you're playing with your destiny." My thoughts were racing a hundred miles an hour. I pulled into the parking lot and ran up the stairs to my apartment. I pushed open the door and headed straight to my bedroom and my Bible. I flipped through the pages until I found the passage Pastor Tim had asked me to read—2 Timothy 2:22: "Flee from youthful passions, and pursue righteousness, faith, love, and peace, along with those who call on the Lord from a pure heart."

As I read the verse, it was like the secrets of my heart were being exposed. There was nowhere to hide. I felt as if God were examining my heart under a microscope, revealing things I'd tried to keep hidden for so long. The very reason I went to the church that night was to fulfill the desires of my flesh. This Scripture was revealing my inner motives. Now that I'd been caught, I knew I had to make a decision: Would I continue to live a self-centered "Christian" life, or would I surrender myself completely to Jesus?

That night I tossed and turned in bed. All I heard, over and over, were Tim's parting words: "Jason, you're playing with your destiny. You're playing with your destiny." God was chasing my heart and I could feel it. My inner wrestling finally gave way to sleep as darkness faded into morning.

Facing the Truth

I woke up tired but excited. I couldn't think of anything except the events of the previous evening. I knew God was getting ready to do something in my life, but I had no idea what it was. That evening I attended a service at the same church. I tried to listen to the sermon, but all I could think about was what had happened the night before. After the service I looked for Pastor Tim and finally found him down near the front.

"Hey, I read the Scripture in 2 Timothy," I blurted out.

His reply was courteous but to the point. "Really? What did it mean to you as you read it?" he inquired. We sat down and began to talk. I told him how his challenge to me had shaken me up. I shared my background—about growing up as a pastor's kid and about what it was like to have always been in youth group.

After listening to me tell about my life, Pastor Tim began to talk. Every word pierced me with conviction. He said something I will never forget: "Salvation is free, but it will cost you everything." I'd known for a long time that I needed to surrender my life completely to Christ, but I was scared—scared to give up control and to not trust in myself. I thought that by surrendering my life to Christ I'd miss out on what the world had to offer.

That night I was ready for a transformation. My life had always revolved around me—my voice, my career, my desires. I had called Jesus "Lord" since I was little, but in reality I was the one seeking to be in control. I'd been content to allow God access to a part of my life—as if I were giving God His little box to fill. Now I knew things needed to be different. He wanted to control the whole thing.

Pastor Tim put his arm around my shoulders and gripped me with a large hand. "Jason," he said, "if this is what you truly desire, then you need to pray and repent for living a halfhearted Christianity." I felt like I'd forgotten how to pray. Imagine! Me—a church kid—forgetting how to pray. It felt that way because I knew this prayer was huge. This was about placing my life in the hands of Jesus. It was an all-or-nothing moment.

I bowed my head and started to pray. Soon my words were mingled with tears as a flood of emotion and desire poured out of my heart. I'd never been so broken before the Lord. I was truly sorry for the ways I had failed Him, sorry to the point of giving up control. This wasn't like the many times before when I'd half-repented of something, knowing that I'd be back the next week doing the very same thing. This time it was for real—it was about living for Jesus.

As I sat there praying, I saw a picture in my mind of the cross and heard the voice of God saying, "I love you. This is what I did for you." I've heard about the cross since my earliest years in Sunday school, but that night my eyes were opened to the reality of Jesus Christ dying for me. For Jason. For the first time, I realized that even as He was dying on the cross, I was on His mind. He endured the pain and agony because He loved me. In my mind's eye, I could see the blood of Jesus flowing down from His hands and feet. As I prayed, I felt God cleansing me of all my sin.

I found myself praying, "Lord, why would You do this for me? Who am I that You would give Your life for Jason?" I realized for the first time how utterly corrupt I was and how desperately I needed Him to control my life.

That evening I repented for all of the lust and pride that had saturated my heart. I asked Him to forgive me for serving Him halfheartedly. I couldn't give enough of myself. I felt as if for years I'd been standing on the edge of a cliff with God standing beneath me, His arms wide open. For so long I'd been too scared to jump. That night, on a church pew with my new friend Pastor Tim, I finally decided to take the leap.

A Fresh Start

The next morning I woke up and literally felt like a new person. "Why didn't I do this a long time ago?" I asked myself. It was time to go back on tour, so I packed my bags and headed to the bus to meet the guys. I felt so different—like a brand-new me. I jumped on the bus and greeted everybody, secretly wondering if they could see on my face how radically I'd changed on the inside. If they did notice, they didn't say anything.

The long drive to our next city gave me time to reflect on the previous two days. I gazed out the window at yellow cornfields and autumn leaves, my mind trying to wrap itself around the events that had just taken place. I decided I couldn't put the experience into words. All I could do was accept it and confirm it by immediately starting to read the Bible.

I remember thinking, *This is how Adam and Eve must have felt when they walked with God in the garden.* Their relationship with God had been perfect until the moment they ate the forbidden fruit. Yet even after their sin, God walked in the garden and called for them by name. He didn't give up on them but called them out from their hiding place into the light of His presence. That's what God had done for me. He didn't leave me alone. Even when my heart was cold and callous, God was continually pursuing me. He called me out—He drew me into the light.

I spent hours on the bus reading my Bible. I couldn't get enough of God's Word. We reached our concert destination the next day, and I was pumped. I couldn't wait to get on stage and sing, but now my motivation was completely different. I had a fire burning in my heart—a fire to sing for God's glory, not mine. During the first half of the tour, my focus had been on the wrong things—my clothes, my voice, the applause of the audience, how many looks I could get during the show. Sound like Jesus was getting all the glory? Yeah, right! Jason wanted all the glory. It was all about me.

Now, however, it was all about Jesus. This time when I introduced songs, I wouldn't just say, "Hey, we're Plus One and God loves you." Now it was different. I actually had something to say; my life had been changed by the power of God. My heart was full of Jesus Christ, and it flowed over into my speaking and singing.

The fire kindled that Halloween night still burns in my heart. It wasn't just a flash-in-the-pan emotional experience. And though I'll be the first to admit that I'm far from perfect, my life has been changed from the inside out. I now have an insatiable hunger for the Bible. Since the night Pastor Tim and I prayed, he has discipled me and taught me how to walk with God. Even now we talk on the phone nearly every day. And just like the night we first met, he still doesn't let me get away with anything less than God's best.

This book is about change. Real change. Heart change. God did it in my life, and He continues the process every day. How about you? Are you at a point where you need a God-sized change in your life? If you don't know Jesus Christ as your Lord and Savior, then that's the first step you need to take. I sincerely hope that my story gives you the desire to meet Him personally. If you already know Him, then I trust this book will persuade you to surrender your entire life to His control.

Let's go on the journey together.

Falling and Rededicating— A Cycle

I grabbed my bag, threw it over my shoulder, and stepped into the van. Making my way to the back, I slumped down into a seat near some good friends. We laughed and told jokes as the engine roared to life and the scenery outside became a passing blur.

As the trip continued, some of us slipped on earphones and listened to music; others were intent on flirting with someone of the opposite sex; and a few rested their head against a window and tried to catch a nap before reaching our destination. It was all about having fun and getting ready for a good time.

No, I'm not describing our Plus One tour bus (aren't you glad?). I'm describing what it was like to go away for a church youth retreat or youth convention. I should know— I've been to plenty of them. Maybe you have too. In my mind, weekends like these (regardless of their beginnings) can be summed up in two words: spiritual high.

The vans would pull into the retreat center, and everyone would unload, stretching their legs before gathering their stuff and settling into a room or cabin. After shooting hoops or hanging out, we'd eat dinner and then get ready for the first meeting of the weekend.

The service would start with music, with most of us just standing there, trying to act cool. Before long, however, the lights, music, and atmosphere would get us charged up, and soon we would forget our egos and get into the experience. Little by little the spiritual mood would escalate, so that by the end of the worship time, we'd be bouncing off the walls. Everyone would be going crazy—it felt incredible to worship God.

By this time everyone would have forgotten about those around them, and the Spirit would be moving, speaking to individual hearts. Then came the speaker. At all the retreats I've ever attended, the speaker would usually be half preacher, half aerobics leader. He would jump around on stage, using full-body motion to get his point across. It always seemed to work; the messages would hit me right between the eyes.

No retreat was complete without an altar call. This was the moment to do business with God. Most everyone would jump out of their seat and run to the front, repenting for every wrong deed committed since the previous retreat months before.

Even the coldest, most rebellious heart seemed to melt during these weekend retreats. We would meet God in a fresh way, and we could feel His touch deep inside our hearts. The weekend was a supercharger to our walk with God. By the end of two or three days, nobody wanted to leave and return to the real world. Yet we'd reluctantly pack our bags and make the long drive, our voices growing hoarse from singing praise songs the whole way home. I would always come back from these weekends ready to change the world for Christ.

The Highs and Lows

As much as I enjoyed the spiritual mountaintops, the excitement for God didn't last long. After several weeks I'd usually find myself back in the same old spiritual ruts.

I was like a guy with two prom dates who leaves one girl at the table and says, "I'll be right back. Just hang here for awhile and I'll get us something to drink." Then he rushes over to where his other date is sitting, spends a few minutes with her, and then makes an excuse to get back to the first girl. Kind of stupid, right? Sooner or later the guy's going to be found out. He'll eventually say or do something that will blow his cover, or the girls will figure it out on their own. That's kind of what I was trying to do with God. I'd sit at His table for awhile and talk the talk, then excuse myself and go hang out at sin's table. Of course I'd always come back to God, full of regret and remorse, not realizing that my heart was growing colder each time I ventured away from His presence.

For several years this was the routine that characterized my life: a cycle of rededication—falling—rededication—falling. To those who knew me, my spiritual walk must have resembled a yo-yo, except every time I fell, I seemed to go farther and farther down. Over time my heart became so cold toward God that I was completely apathetic toward Him and church. I didn't really care anymore. I was going to do my own thing. My cold heart led to apathy, and apathy led me down the path of rebellion.

Sounds Familiar to Me

Recently I received an E-mail from one of our fans. She was honest in telling me about her walk with God; her experience is not at all uncommon for those of us who've grown up in church. Here are some excerpts from her letter. See if you can relate to her story.

> I've been a Christian since I was six. I don't know how much you can truly know about Christianity when you are so young, but you know what I mean.

Throughout my life, I feel like I've been on this roller coaster when it comes to my faith. I've been up and down so many times that I've lost track. I don't know if you've ever been on a coaster so many times that it starts to get boring, but that's sort of the point I'm at right now. I've ridden this ride too many times to count; it all seems sort of redundant to me. I guess I've lived that "normal" teenage Christian life. You're flaming-on-fire [for Christ] on Saturday nights and Sunday mornings. And you're even more on fire when you're out camping in the remote woods, but once you get off the "mountain," you're back where you started—one foot in the world and one foot out. I haven't been the perfect little Christian girl that people make me out to be. I've made my mistakes— a lot, in fact. My past is not something I am entirely proud of. And this takes me to where I am now. I'd like to call myself—at the moment—"stuck" in the middle. I'm not sure where to go now or which way is up. I've been pulled and tossed around so many times that I've lost my sense of direction. I've been praying and praying and really trying to be as patient as pos- sible. I've just basically been asking the Lord to show me what to do.

I can relate to her story because for years I, too, found myself stuck on the same emotional roller coaster. I did well when I was at church, and I was there every Sunday morning, Sunday evening, and Wednesday night. But those three hours each week were the only hours I would spend worshiping God or even looking at my Bible. My walk with God was totally event-driven. I wasn't seeking to live in God's presence all day every day. Instead, I lived for the emotional highs and the spiritual events that would give them to me.

Now I know there's a better way to walk with God, and it's not dependent upon my feelings. To get off the emotional roller coaster, we have to take some steps and make some choices.

Repentance is one of the first choices we need to make.

The Road to Repentance

It was in my junior year of high school that I began to look at the world with envy in my eyes. Up until then, I had been a pretty good kid. I sang in church, went to youth group, and by all outward appearances was doing OK spiritually. That year, though, became a year of new decisions. My involvement in sports meant that many of my friends were non-Christians, and I would hear these guys tell locker-room stories about partying on the weekends. Up to this point, I'd never really considered joining them in what I knew was wrong.

Yet as my heart grew cold, their lifestyle became more and more attractive as they talked about the fun they were having. It wasn't long until I began to rationalize their behavior. "What in the world am I doing to have fun?" I'd say to myself, sarcastically. "Let's see—oh yeah, I go to church every time the doors are open. Wow, I'm having a ball! This has got to change."

CHAPTER THREE

I thought about it for a couple weeks, debating whether I wanted to take the plunge. I knew going to parties and drinking was sin, but I was getting good at rationalizing poor behavior. "After all," I'd say to myself, "if my friends are having this much fun, it can't be *that* bad. Besides, if I never try it, then I'll always be curious about what I'm missing." I was talking myself into doing something that I knew was completely wrong.

One Friday night after a basketball game, a friend told me he was going to a party. I thought to myself, *Man, that sounds fun. I never drank before, but maybe tonight I'll try it.* I could sense the Spirit of God whispering caution to my soul. I knew that this would be testing God and His patience with me, but by that time, I didn't really care. I shook off the Spirit's voice and took the plunge. I went to the party and got drunk for the first time in my life.

At first I remember thinking how much fun I was having. I was flush with an exhilaration I'd never felt before— the initial rush of excitement that comes with doing something forbidden. Yet here I was in a place I'd never dreamed I'd be, acting no better than those around me who had little or no knowledge of God. Yet I was a Christian. How had this happened?

At that point I could have turned around and determined never to go out partying again, but I didn't. My heart had become so cold and hard that I barely cared about the truth of my situation. The party scene wasn't really that much fun, but I somehow became stuck, not knowing how to back myself out of the mess I was in. This began a season in my life of apathy, wrong choices, and an obvious distance from God.

At the same time, my love for singing was fading. Focused on so many other things, I just lost interest in using my voice. It's funny how all the things I had enjoyed before—going to church, leading worship, hanging out with kids from the youth group—became less and less important. I began to ignore my family, my church—even the fact that my dad was a pastor. All these things no longer had an effect on me. I violated the trust of those who were closest to me, and for a long time, it didn't bother me in the least.

Partial Repentance

By the summer before my senior year, I was ready for a change. I'd been living the party scene for several months and finally understood that I was making a fool of myself. I stopped going to parties and drinking, realizing that this lifestyle was taking me nowhere. I told God I was sorry for what I'd been doing, but the change came because of feeling foolish, not because I was ready to surrender my life to Christ.

For the next year or two I worked at not committing any more big sins, but my heart was still torn in two. Wanting the best of both worlds, I was afraid that if I sold out completely to God, all the fun in this world would pass me by. I decided to remain in control of my life. Sure, God could have His little section of my heart, but ultimately I'd make my own decisions. My repentance was halfhearted. And one thing's for sure—God was not impressed.

True Repentance

That was the condition of my heart until that Halloween night when I met Pastor Tim. Without realizing it, God had finally brought me to a place where I was ready to give it all up for Him. I was tired of trying to figure out everything on my own. I was done with living a life of compromise. I just couldn't do it anymore. When I sat with Pastor Tim that next evening and poured out my heart to God, it was true repentance. I was no longer holding on to any options—this time, it was all or nothing.

What does it mean to repent before God? Does it mean to feel sorry for doing wrong things? Sure, that's part of it. Yet sorrow alone isn't enough. I often felt sorry for doing bad things, but not sorry enough to make huge changes in my life.

In 2 Corinthians 7:10, the Bible compares godly grief and worldly grief: "For godly grief produces a repentance not to be regretted and leading to salvation, but worldly grief produces death." My grief usually came from the harsh results of sin or because I was in need and wanted something from God. If my conscience was guilty, I would tell God I was sorry. Yet my sorrow was based only on regret, not on true repentance.

In the Bible the word *repent* means "to turn." Someone who truly repents of his sin will make an all-out effort to change his behavior.

Imagine you had a friend who kept stealing money from you, and one day you caught him in the act. If your friend said he was sorry, but then kept stealing from you again and again, would you be convinced that he was serious about changing his behavior? Not at all. At that point, his words would become empty—repentance with no fruit is not repentance at all.

True repentance brings fruit—that's how we know it's real. In Acts 26:20, Paul preached that people "should repent and turn to God, and do works worthy of repentance." Jesus said much the same thing when He talked to the crowds in Matthew 7:17, 20: "Every good tree produces good fruit, but a bad tree produces bad fruit. . . . So you'll recognize them by their fruit."

I'd prayed the prayer of repentance many times before, yet never accompanied it with real life change. This time, however, fruit happened. I immediately went home and started reading the Bible. I started memorizing Scripture. I began to pray. Over time I changed the way I talked, no longer using some off-color slang that would sometimes permeate my speech. My entire attitude was and is different than it used to be, all because I ran to the Light and asked God to completely take over my life. It's been a dramatic change.

So what is repentance? Imagine a two-way road with a car heading in one direction. It then stops, pulls a U-turn, and begins to go the other way. A 180-degree turn: That's the biblical meaning behind repentance.

When I look back at how I was living, a guy named Esau comes to mind. He and his brother, Jacob, lived hundreds of years ago (their story is told in the Book of Genesis—the first book of the Bible). Esau was a hunter. He loved the outdoors and everything about the hunting lifestyle. Jacob, however, was a homebody. He preferred to hang out around the house with Mom.

One day Esau went hunting and came back famished. He said to his brother, "Hey, Jacob. Make me some of that special soup of yours. I've got to have something to eat!"

Jacob knew a good opportunity when he saw one, so he replied, "No problem. I'll fix you all the soup you want if you'll let me have your birthright." In those days, the birthright was a big deal; it was intended to go to the firstborn son (Esau, in this case), and was the way a father would give material and spiritual blessings to his oldest boy. However, Esau didn't care about the blessings or about God—all he wanted was to fill his empty stomach. For a bowl of soup, he sold his valuable birthright to his younger brother, Jacob. (Read Genesis 25:29–34 to get the whole story.)

That's what I was doing—I was giving up God's best for a cheap thrill. God had given me the gift of singing and a chance to use that gift for Him. Yet I was throwing it away for the temporary excitement of what sin could offer. A lose-lose situation, for sure.

That's why that prayer of repentance with Pastor Tim was so different from all the times I'd repented before. I had prayed the same words many times, but now they were accompanied by godly grief and a willingness to completely turn from the lifestyle I'd been living.

After we'd finished praying, I looked up at Pastor Tim and said, "I can't do this on my own. I can't go back on the road without being accountable to someone. Up to this point, my dad has been my pastor, but now that I'm away from home, I want you to be my pastor. I'm submitting myself to your authority. Teach me how to become a man of God."

Pastor Tim looked at me and said, "OK, Jason—I'll be your pastor." That was the beginning of a powerful relationship that God has used and is still using to change my life.

God uses mature people to help others grow in Christ. Sometimes we call these people mentors. There's no better way to grow in your faith than to find a mature person who will mentor you in your Christian walk.

Joining the Band and Finding a Mentor

A couple of years ago on a Sunday morning, I'd just crawled out of bed to get ready for church. Everybody at our house was in their normal routine—my dad was walking around singing, mom was making cinnamon rolls, and my brothers and sister were just pulling themselves out of their own warm covers to greet the day.

Dad walked into my room with a not-so-unusual request: "Jason, how about singing during the service this morning?" I said, "No problem," and immediately started fumbling through some music tapes to find a song appropriate for the morning service.

Music has always been a part of my life. I started singing in church at age twelve and have sung more solos at church than I can count. My mom would often go to the Christian bookstore and get song tracks for me to sing with. I'd sing songs by BeBe Wynans, Stephen Curtis Chapman,

Fred Hammond, Michael English, and lots of others. Now when I'm around these artists at music festivals or at the Dove Awards, it feels kind of funny, but also pretty cool because just a few years ago, I was singing their songs in church.

That Sunday morning I found the tape for "His Eye Is on the Sparrow," which at the time was a family favorite. I knew that we had a special guest by the name of Rich Wilkerson speaking for church that morning, and I was looking forward to being a part of the service.

As the church service began, I played the drums for worship. Then I sang with the choir before stepping forward and singing my solo. That's part of the luxury of being a pastor's kid: A little bit of talent gets stretched a long way. There was never a lack of opportunity to perform for the congregation.

The solo went well, and the rest of the service finished without a hitch. After church I talked with Rich in my dad's office, and he said, "Jason, I really enjoyed your singing this morning. I've got a second cousin named Nate who is also a singer. He's about your age. Nate is in a band with three other guys, and they're looking for one more person to fill a spot. Jason, you're the perfect guy for this. I think you should definitely try out for this new group."

Rich went on to explain that it was a boy band of five guys. He said they had originally found all five members, but one of them had recently dropped out for personal

25

reasons. The guys needed to find a fifth member to complete the band, and Rich was sure I'd be a perfect fit.

I remember thinking to myself, *Wow, that would be pretty cool.* I'd never sung with a group of guys my age, so the idea of being with four other guys who loved to sing and minister sounded like an awesome idea. I told him that I was very interested and would love to pursue the opportunity.

Later that day Rich gave Nate a call, saying, "I've found your guy." The next day I mailed some audio- and video-tapes to Nate and his family. Within three days I had heard from their manager, and a week later I was on a plane to meet the group in San Francisco. This was the beginning of a whirlwind, and, man, was I nervous!

A Dream Come True

The whole time the plane was in the air, my mind was whirling: *I wonder what the guys will think of me? Am I good enough for this, or will I have to return home disappointed?*

The group's manager met me at the airport, and we drove straight to where the band was practicing their choreography. I walked in and saw the guys dancing, learning a new routine. To be honest, it struck me as kind of funny. I had never danced before in my life, other than attending some school dances where all the guys would act cool and stand around with their hands in their pockets.

This was definitely out of my comfort zone, but I sat down and watched while they finished the rehearsal.

We all grabbed a bite to eat before heading back to the apartment and on to vocal rehearsal. I remember sitting in the car and feeling incredibly nervous. The guys were all very friendly, though, and they put me at ease. When we got to the manager's house and started to sing, it felt like we had been together all our lives. The blend of our voices was magical. It was fun to be around guys who sang and were good at it.

The manager called me upstairs after we'd rehearsed for awhile. "Well, Jason, what do you think about all of this?" He was curious about everything I'd experienced so far that day. I expressed how much fun I was having and that it was really feeling good.

"Well," he began, "I've got to talk to the guys, but I think you can go home pretty much assured that you're in the group. Basically, you've got a week to pack your things and then move out here to live. That is, if you want to."

I could barely believe my ears. This was a dream come true. I'd known from childhood that I wanted to be involved in music but never imagined that it would be as a recording artist, traveling around the world and singing in front of thousands of people.

I flew home the next morning, arriving just in time to play my last high school football game. Life was going to be very different—very soon.

Leaving Home

My parents and I talked long and hard about what was happening. We spent that next week praying and seeking God to make sure that we were making the right decision. In many ways it seemed too good to be true. Yet the more we prayed about it, the more we sensed that God was the One opening this door. We decided as a family that we couldn't let this opportunity pass me by.

This decision meant leaving school, sports, friends, church, family—everything that was secure and familiar. I was moving out, no longer a child living under Mom and Dad's roof. It was a huge step, and it left us all nervous, excited, and more than a little scared.

The night before I left, my parents walked into my room and gave me a giant hug. "Jason, you know we've been praying about this," said Dad. "We feel like we'd be disobeying God if we didn't let you go." I know it wasn't easy on them, especially on my mom. After all, her baby was leaving home, and she wasn't crazy about my living so far away. Yet my parents were determined to obey God no matter how they felt inside.

My family and I cried together at the airport the next morning before I boarded the plane. It wasn't that I thought I'd never see them again, but it was obvious that a chapter in our lives was closing forever and that a new journey was opening up before us. I walked onto the plane, sat in my seat, and bawled like a baby. Still, it was the beginning of a new journey, an opportunity to trust the Lord on my own.

Big Adjustments

I arrived in San Francisco just two weeks after hearing about Plus One from Rich Wilkerson. Believe me, life in the big city was different from life in the small Indiana town where I'd grown up. Mom was no longer there to do my laundry; my little brother and I were no longer sharing a room; and Dad and I couldn't go shoot hoops anytime we felt like it. Everything I'd ever known was now behind me, far away in Indiana.

During those initial days of joining the group, my walk with the Lord was doing well. I had been on a choir tour the previous summer, and through it God had impacted my life so that my relationship with Him was going great. With Plus One, I'd practice vocals and choreography during the week, then minister at local churches every Sunday. It didn't take long for me to bond with the other guys; all of us had grown up in church and three of us were pastors' kids, so we had a lot in common. It was obvious from the start that these were great guys, and within the first week, I think we knew everything there was to know about each other.

Then something began to happen that I didn't expect. As the weeks and months passed by, I sensed that I wasn't as on fire for God as when I'd first joined the group. Yes, we were in church every Sunday, but it was mostly to perform, not to be fed by the Word of God. The change was barely noticeable, but real. As guys, we would talk about spiritual things, but there wasn't a strong accountability among us because we were still getting to know each other. We'd share our struggles and temptations, which was helpful, but overall I became more independent than I'd ever been before. We had no limits. No boundaries. No one told us what to do and what not to do. Sure, there were people around us who encouraged us to stay grounded and keep on track, but I was free to live the life I wanted to live.

After three and a half months, we moved to Los Angeles to record our first album. The excitement of it all was starting to wear off, and worse yet, I wasn't spending much time with the Lord praying or reading the Bible. The studio work went well, but inside I began to feel frustrated, even angry at myself. I was mad because I knew I wasn't where I should be with God but was too prideful to admit that I was falling away.

When the record was released in May 2000, things only got busier. We moved to Nashville and began preparing for the promo tour. We went on the road just before the release, which meant I had even less time for spiritual things. I know that God was using us to minister His truth to people through our concerts, but inside I felt I didn't have much to give. Having become spiritually dry, I needed God to break the apathy that was stifling me on the inside.

Enter Accountability

That's how I was feeling the night I met Pastor Tim. I was in desperate need of someone to get into my life—someone to challenge me and mentor me in the Word. That's why my mouth dropped open when Tim took me aside and started telling me what I needed to hear. I knew that God was answering the hidden prayer of my heart—He was giving me someone who would teach me how to walk with Him.

In the Bible we see that the apostle Paul was a mentor to younger men. Check out what he says in 1 Thessalonians 2:7b–8: "We were gentle among you, as a nursing mother nurtures her own children. We cared so much for you that we were pleased to share with you not only the gospel of God but also our own lives, because you had become dear to us."

God used Pastor Tim in my life in incredible ways. Here was a man I could look up to—a man who had experienced many of the same things in life that I was going through. When I looked in his eyes, I saw a passion for Jesus, the same kind of passion that I longed to have in my life. Yet he's been much more than just a role model to me—he's taught me what it means to be a godly man walking with Christ. I thought I knew it all already, but now I see that I've got a long way to go. Pastor Tim is willing to walk with me along the way, asking me tough questions and helping me to find the right answers.

Before I met Pastor Tim, I was floundering like an aimless ship on the waves of the sea, tossed around by whatever wind was blowing by me at the time. Opening up to Pastor Tim has brought stability to my walk with God because our relationship is based on the Word of God. I am accountable to a godly person who helps me live life in a godly manner.

Getting Your Own Mentor

The first step in getting a spiritual mentor is to recognize your need for one. When I was seventeen years old, I was sure I knew all there was to know about life. I was a lone-ranger Christian, convinced that I didn't need anyone to help me grow spiritually. I thought this would bring me freedom, but it only kept me in bondage. I was in bondage because I wasn't in a position to see my weaknesses, and as I hid my weaknesses from myself and others, I deluded myself into thinking I was spiritually mature. This caused my spiritual growth to be severely stunted.

Now that I've opened my life to Pastor Tim, I couldn't go back to any other way of living. I have found incredible freedom in being honest and transparent with another person. It has caused me to dig deep into God's Word. It has kept me from becoming proud.

Imagine if football or basketball leagues did away with coaches. It would result in chaos because players need coaches to give them direction. When I look back on the sports I played in high school, I know that I would never have reached my full potential without the encouragement and discipline I received from my coaches.

The same is true in the spiritual life. A mentor is like a coach—someone who will help you reach your full potential in your Christian walk. In fact, it's not likely that anyone can attain maturity in his walk with Christ without someone to challenge and encourage him spiritually. We are made to need other people. We are made to need a mentor.

When I look into Pastor Tim's eyes, I see purity, integrity, and a passion for God's Word. I see a man who is up every morning before the sun rises, seeking God's face in prayer. I see a man whose kids love God with all their heart. This is the type of man I want to be.

My hero is not some sports star or movie celebrity. My hero is my pastor. Who is your hero? Find someone who practices the kind of life with Christ that you would like to live. Then ask that person to be your mentor, and watch God work.

Learning the Word

Immediately after I met Pastor Tim, he gave me an assignment: Start memorizing Scripture.

I had never really known how to approach the Bible. Whenever I wanted to read it, I would hold my Bible in front of me, close my eyes, open it, and start reading wherever my finger landed. I really had no idea of where to start or how to read it methodically. Sometimes I would try to read in the Old Testament, but to be honest, most of the stories seemed dusty and old. I would quickly get bored. To me, the Bible didn't seem relevant. The only reason I would read it was so I could say I read it.

The first time I was powerfully impacted by the Bible was the night Pastor Tim told me to look up 2 Timothy 2:22. As I read that verse over and over, I found it hitting home like never before. For the first time, I felt as if God was speaking directly to me. That evening was the beginning of a new adventure—the adventure of getting to know God through His Word.

CHAPTER FIVE

Pastor Tim challenged me to memorize that verse in 2 Timothy. *No way,* I thought. *This verse is huge. I can't do this.* It was a whole two lines long. I hadn't memorized Scripture for years, not since I was a kid in Sunday school. I didn't think I could do it, but Pastor Tim insisted that I try and told me to give him a call when I was done.

I worked on that verse night and day until I finally had it in my mind. Excited, I called Pastor Tim, ready to show him that I'd been working hard.

"OK, Pastor, I've got it. Listen to this." I started the verse and got about halfway through before I began to forget some words. "Uh, uh. Oh, man. What is that word?" I began to stutter.

Pastor Tim stopped me. "Jason, wait a minute. You don't sing your songs like that, do you? All chopped up and broken, not knowing the lyrics? No way—you know those lyrics backward and forward. That's how the Word should be—like a song. Smooth like a song."

He was right. I hung up and went to work again, this time getting it down smooth. I called him a couple days later and recited the verse perfectly.

"Great, Jason," he said with an encouraging voice. "Now, let's go for 1 Thessalonians 4:1–12."

I couldn't believe my ears. "Twelve verses? You've got to be kidding, Pastor. That's crazy. I can't do that!" I was trying my best to get out of it, but he was persistent. He had a phrase that he'd use on me whenever I complained about the challenge he'd given. He'd say, "Do you really want to walk this way?" That phrase got me every time. I'd always rise to the challenge, even though there were times when I felt like giving up.

He gave me a deadline—four days—to memorize all those verses. I went to work immediately. I carried my Bible with me everywhere. When I couldn't carry my Bible, I carried the verses with me on three-by-five cards; I wrote them on adhesive notes and plastered them on my bunk in the tour bus. I even listened to the Bible on CD—anything to cement the verses in my mind. Amazingly, after four days I'd memorized all twelve verses. I couldn't believe it. I called Pastor Tim and recited the whole passage to him, proud as a peacock. I could tell he was thrilled with my hard work.

Now I had two portions of Scripture under my belt. The Word was becoming fun, and it didn't seem as difficult to understand as it had before. With Tim's help, I was actually reading portions of the Bible that directly touched my life. I wasn't fumbling through the pages anymore with my eyes closed. Now I was reading passages that dealt directly with what was going on inside of me.

After a few weeks I began to notice changes in my life. The Word of God was cleansing me, purifying my thoughts. For so long it had seemed that living a life of purity in this world was impossible. I would rationalize impure thoughts and actions by thinking, *Society is too evil. Immorality is everywhere. There's no way I can live pure in the midst of this world.*

Yet the more I focused my mind on Scripture, the more my mind was cleansed from impurity. Not only did my thoughts begin to change, but the hidden desires of my heart began to change as well. For the first time in my life, I began to enjoy reading my Bible. It was no longer a chore—it became a delight!

Pastor Tim wasn't done raising the bar, however. One day we were talking on the phone and he said, "You're doing great, Jason. But are you ready to raise it to the next level?" Full of a newfound confidence, I said, "Sure, bring it on."

Pastor Tim dropped the bomb: "All right. Memorize Romans 8." I thought that would be easy—a few verses from Romans 8 wouldn't be too bad. "No, Jason, not a few verses. The whole chapter."

I dropped the phone.

"What in the world. I can't do that. That's impossible. There's no way." I gave him every excuse I could think of, but he stood firm. "You'll get it," he said knowingly. I could tell he was smiling on the other end of the phone. I thought he was crazy.

I began reading Romans 8 over and over. The first line hit me hard: "Therefore, no condemnation now exists for those in Christ Jesus." That got my attention. Then the next few verses went on to explain how we are to be led by the Spirit of God, not our sinful nature. Wow, this was good stuff. I had always excused my sin by saying that I was made to sin. God knows I'm going to sin, so why not just give in and do what comes naturally? That was one of the excuses I used all the time. This passage, though, was hitting me between the eyes. It nailed me, taking away my flimsy excuses. It was telling me that if I set my mind on the Spirit, then I could live by the Spirit and not by the flesh. There was no reason to carelessly give in to fleshly appetites.

God was weeding stuff out of me, replacing it with seeds of righteousness and purity. I began to think differently and act differently. It was all because I was falling in love with the Word of God. It was transforming my life, my ideas, my everything. The Bible went from being this big, black book I didn't understand to a living book that was changing my life. It was transforming me into a different person, and I loved it. I could really relate to Romans 12:2: "Do not be conformed to this age, but be transformed by the renewing of your mind, so that you may discern what is the good, pleasing, and perfect will of God."

Joy in Memorization?

Memorizing Scripture takes hard work and discipline. It's not something that comes easily to me, and it probably won't for you either. So why do it? If you're in school, you probably have lots of homework. Why add something else to your busy schedule, especially something that takes time, discipline, and such concentrated effort?

I know that there are some people reading this chapter who are adamant that they can't memorize. Period. Getting homework done on time is difficult enough, but memorizing portions of the Bible? *Come on*, someone might be thinking at this point. *I'm not a bookworm type of person.*

It's amazing to me that people who find every excuse possible to not memorize Scripture can often quote their favorite movie in its entirety. Most teens can turn on the radio and sing every lyric of every song for hours, yet they would come up empty if they were asked to quote more than two or three Bible verses by heart. And they wonder why their spiritual life is weak. Consider this: If you fill your mind with the things of the world, why would you expect to be able to live a victorious Christian life?

Ever since God got hold of my heart, I've been frequently asked by young people, "What's your secret for maintaining a strong Christian walk with God?" My answer is simple: Live a life based on the Word of God. It's easy for young people to think, *I'll never be like Jason. He's different from me. I'll never enjoy the kind of walk with God he has.* The Bible, however, says that God doesn't show favoritism. You, too, can know God and have an impact wherever you are. I'm not a superstar Christian with a fast track to God; I'm an average nineteen-year-old guy who decided to pick up God's Word and read it. And most importantly, I started to believe it.

So why take the time? If memorizing Scripture requires discipline and hard work, why even bother? Read on for a few reasons from my own experience.

Memorizing Scripture will cleanse your mind. Psalm 119:9 says, "How can a young man keep his way pure? By keeping it according to Your word."

Just two verses later, in verse 11, it says, "Your word I have treasured in my heart, that I may not sin against You."

As I began to commit verses to memory, I found that all I was thinking about was the Word. My mind became occupied with things I was learning from the Bible, leaving less time for my mind to become contaminated by ungodly things around me. The Word was replacing all the normal, natural thoughts of lust, pride, and guilt.

The more I got into God's Word, the more I began to crave it. After getting the memory assignments from Pastor Tim, I found myself spending time in my bunk with the Bible open instead of sitting in front of the television watching MTV. Sometimes I would race to my bunk after signing autographs and start reading. I fell so much in love with my Bible that I would literally sleep with it under my pillow. I'm nineteen years old, so it's not like I need to sleep with a security blanket. It's just that I love having my Bible near me. I love its flippable pages and the way it feels in my hands. I even love the smell of its well-worn leather cover. Most of all, I love to read it. I love the truth it contains on every one of its pages.

Jesus says, "For where your treasure is, there your heart will be also" (Matthew 6:21). Where is your treasure? Do you pursue the fleshly things this world has to offer, or are you consumed with the Word of God? If you are focused on God's Word, you won't be filling your mind with the junk of this world. In fact, there's no way to stay pure of mind without a commitment to reading and memorizing the Word of God.

Memorizing Scripture will help you resist temptation. Have you ever felt helpless against temptations? I sure have. For a long time I wasn't sure if it was even possible to overcome many of the temptations that came my way. You know the feeling—some temptations hit us so hard that we surrender with little or no fight. We feel horrible after we give in, and we promise to never fall in that area again—that is, until the next time it comes our way. I've learned that it *is* possible to overcome temptation by renewing my mind daily in God's Word.

For instance, in Matthew 4 we see how the Word of God is used in fighting temptation. Jesus had just finished fasting for forty days. The devil knew He was hungry and weary, so he tempted Jesus with food when His body was weak. Satan is a master at hitting each of us in our weakest areas. He was trying to bring down the Son of God before His ministry even got started.

What amazes me about this story is that Jesus Himself used the Bible to resist Satan. Three times Satan came against Jesus, and three times Satan was defeated by the Word of God. Think about it: Jesus was perfect and could not sin, yet He quoted Scripture to resist the devil. How much more, then, should we who are weak and imperfect know and quote the Bible to resist temptation.

Hebrews 4:12a says, "For the word of God is living and effective and sharper than any two-edged sword." God has given us a powerful weapon to use against evil. All we have to do is take it up and use it. I'm learning that when impure or evil thoughts come to mind, those thoughts will go away when I immediately focus my mind on the Word. It sounds simple, but it works every time. The Bible is a mighty weapon against temptation.

Memorizing Scripture increases your passion for the Lord. When we immerse ourselves in the Bible, we can't help but see Jesus more clearly, for the Bible is where Jesus is revealed. I've found that the more I see of Jesus, the more I fall in love with Him. It's that simple. In fact, Scripture says something similar in John 14:21: "The one who has My commandments and keeps them is the one who loves Me. And the one who loves Me will be loved by My Father. I also will love him and will reveal Myself to him."

If you love Jesus, you will desire to keep His commandments. If you don't have much of a desire to read the Bible, then you may not love God as much as you think you do. If you want to love Him more, then spend time getting to know Him through His Word. The Bible is where we can meet Him whenever we desire.

Memorizing Scripture will increase your effectiveness as you serve the Lord. The point of memorizing Scripture is not so we can sit around and quote verses to each other. It is for the purpose of ministry. First, God ministers to us by His Word as it becomes woven into the fabric of our lives. We become changed from the inside out. Then God desires to use each of us to minister to people around us. But without a biblical foundation, we'll have nothing to give.

I'm not saying you need to memorize the entire Bible before God can use you. The key is getting the Word of God into your mind and your heart bit by bit. Memorizing the Word is one of the most effective ways that this can take place. It's impossible to serve the Lord effectively and yet be disconnected from His Word. It just can't happen.

I love my church and my mentors, and I love hearing great men and women of God talk about the Bible. But I also want to know the Word for myself. I want to know what I believe and why I believe it. I want to know why I'm saved, why I should pray a certain way and not another, and why my church does certain things and not others. I want to minister to others out of my own experience with the Lord, not out of someone else's experience or knowledge. I won't be content only with others' interpretation of Scripture. I want to know the Bible for myself.

That's why studying and memorizing the Word is so important.

Getting Started

Please understand that studying and memorizing the Word is a process. It wasn't easy for me to memorize verses when I first began, but the more I tried, the more the Lord helped me. As a young person, I have complete confidence that I will fulfill the good works that God desires to do through me because I am building my life on the Word of God. You can share in this confidence by becoming a disciple of His Word.

Joshua 1:8 puts it this way: "This book of the law shall not depart from your mouth, but you shall meditate on it day and night, so that you may be careful to do according to all that is written in it; for then you will make your way prosperous, and then you will have success."

Rebelling
and Healing

Afew years before I'd met Pastor Tim, I was speeding my car along some country roads. It was a beautiful Saturday afternoon and a bright autumn sun hung overhead. The car radio was playing quietly in the background, but I didn't notice. All I could hear were the harsh voices of regret—voices that played again and again in my mind. I pressed down on the gas pedal, trying to drive some distance between the future and what had happened the night before.

"Am I dreaming?" I muttered to myself. "Oh, God, let me be dreaming." I turned up the radio to drown out my thoughts—anything to keep from reliving what I'd done the previous evening. Yet no matter how fast I drove or how loud I played the radio, I couldn't escape the fact that last night had really happened. I had lost my virginity.

Actually, I had given it away of my own free will. I drove on, thinking about what had taken place. I was angry at myself, at others, and at the culture around me that said sex was no big deal. I had bought the lie, and now I knew better. The guys in the locker room had made it sound so cool, as if anyone who wasn't having sex was an idiot. They didn't tell me that the next morning—this morning—would be full of emptiness, pain, regret, and sorrow. I felt stupid and dirty, like I'd traded the most precious diamond in the world for a cheap, dime-store trinket. I knew I'd been had.

I drove for hours that day, my mind retracing the steps that had brought me to this point of moral failure. I passed by my house and then by the church that was so important to our family. I'd grown up in the shadow of both structures—the lessons learned in each building were lessons of morality, strength, and godly character. I had been instructed to live differently from the world, to resist temptation, to uphold the things my parents taught me, and most important, to obey the Bible.

I knew my failure was not the result of one momentary lapse in judgment. I'd been laying the groundwork for a long time without even realizing it. Many small wayward decisions had carried me to the edge of the abyss. It took only a suitable opportunity to provide the fall.

I thought back to the moment of decision. Warning bells had been blaring in my mind, but I didn't heed them. I disregarded the clear voice of the Holy Spirit, desiring instead to follow my sinful passions rather than the way of purity. I had previously played on the edge to see how far I could go without actually having sex. It was a dangerous game, and it was fun. What I didn't realize, however, was that this game had no winners. I was gambling that I would stay strong when the moment came. I lost the bet.

Listening to the Wrong Voices

Sex is no big deal—at least that's what I'd been led to believe. I wanted to be just like everybody else, and most of the people I looked up to at school were sexually active. I began to wonder why I was holding out. It's no fun feeling like an oddball, especially when your friends are telling you all about their sexual escapades. After awhile, I decided I'd prove to God that I could be my own person, that I could be like everybody else. It wasn't that I didn't know right from wrong; I just didn't care anymore.

As amazing as it seems to me now, I didn't humble myself before God at that point in my life. Rather, I allowed my sexual sin to make me even colder. I had just gone against everything my parents had taught me, but I was too prideful to admit my sin. "I've messed up big time," I told myself, "so I guess it doesn't matter what I do from now on. I might as well enjoy my rebellion as long as I'm here." I should have run from my sin at that point; instead, I embraced it.

This was the beginning of a full-on rebellion. My frustration and feelings of regret led to apathy, and my heart became hardened as the months went by. I found myself troubled by thoughts of worthlessness. I felt like I had nothing left to give, that since I'd opened the forbidden door of premarital sex, there was no going back. I could never be pure again.

Along with the rebellion and the frustration came the overwhelming weight of guilt. I couldn't tell my family for I knew my parents would be hurt beyond words. I didn't even want to tell my friends; out of respect for the girl, I didn't want everybody to know what had happened between us. So I carried the guilt deep inside, trying to keep it from spilling over and becoming visible.

This took place a couple months before my buddy asked me to that first party where I got drunk. I had said no at first, but then I thought about it for awhile. "I've already fallen into sin," I reasoned to myself. "I guess there's nothing left to lose." I'm sure my friends were shocked when I agreed to go. They were even more shocked when I grabbed some alcohol and started drinking. I had never tasted it before, but I was intent on fitting in with the crowd. I tried to act like having a drink in my hand was normal. I drank until I passed out.

The next morning my friends were giddy over how crazy I'd been the night before. I couldn't remember anything about it, but they assured me I'd been the life of the party. It made me feel good. I laughed with the guys and inwardly reveled in how great it felt to finally fit in with my peers. I was still a little sick by the time I went to church on

Sunday. There I was, playing drums and singing in the choir, trying to overcome my first hangover. Sitting on stage, I decided I didn't want to be involved in leading worship anymore. No longer was I going to be a church boy—it was time to experience real life. I knew what church was all about; now I wanted to see what the world had to offer.

Living by the World's Standards

Over the next few months I went to more parties and did more stupid things. Word was getting around that Jason Perry was going out and acting pretty wild. I thought it was cool. That was exactly what I wanted to happen. I wanted to fit in. On Friday and Saturday nights I was out living like the devil, then on Sunday mornings I would listen to my dad's sermons and not blink an eye. I lost all desire to sing and went from leading worship every Sunday to singing only now and then. In the course of just a few months I had changed immensely—at least on the outside. What my friends couldn't see was the turmoil going on beneath the surface. As much as I tried, I just couldn't get comfortable in my new role as a rebel. The conviction in my heart was becoming unbearable.

One night I got home late after being out with friends. It was late—too late—and my parents had long since gone to bed. I opened the front door, trying to keep it from squeaking and waking up my mom. I tiptoed into the bathroom, catching a glimpse of myself in the mirror. My eyes were bloodshot, and I barely recognized the unkempt person staring back at me over the sink.

"Jason, what are you doing?" The words slipped out of my mouth before I knew they were there. "Who are you trying to be? You're throwing away everything—all your dreams, all your gifts. Why are you acting this way?"

The next day was a Sunday. I got up early and got to church in plenty of time. I was ready to make a change, ready to give it all back to the Lord. My dad ended his sermon with an altar call, as he often did, and I was one of the first to make it down front. I got right with God. I asked Him to forgive me for the foolish way I'd been living. Immediately I sensed His cleansing and His forgiveness. A fresh wave of peace rolled over me. It felt so good to be home.

Dealing with the Guilt

Things were going well. I stopped my rebellious lifestyle and began to live a life pleasing to God. Yet I was troubled by something that was stealing my peace—something that went deep, troubling me to the very core of my being: guilt. Not a day went by when I didn't think about how badly I'd messed up. I asked God repeatedly to forgive me for what I'd done, but I wasn't able to shake the guilt.

It was during the quiet moments of the day that I sensed my condemning thoughts. They were telling me over and over again, *You're not forgiven. You're not forgiven.* I couldn't tell if it was Satan whispering things to my mind or if it was just my guilty conscience working overtime. Whatever the source of my thoughts, I became consumed with remorse for the things I had done.

For instance, thoughts about my future wedding day would flash before me. I could picture myself standing before my bride, my dad standing in front of us, performing the ceremony. Yet instead of feeling excitement and happiness, I would be thinking about the fact that I wasn't a virgin. I had robbed my future wife of something precious, and I struggled with the fact that a person besides my bride knew me in a way that should have been reserved only for her.

The images of my failure played frequently in my mind. It was like a black cloud of guilt and condemnation hanging over my head. I felt so dirty. I was sure that no girl would want to be with me once she knew about my past. In fact, I became convinced that I had no chance of ever marrying a girl who had kept herself pure. I knew I didn't deserve anyone like that. I figured it was punishment for the choices I'd made.

The guilt stayed with me even after I joined Plus One. Though I would never lie about my past when asked, I would do my best to avoid the subject as much as possible. I cringed inside when the issue of sexual purity would come up in conversation, even with the guys in the group. I told them about my past, and they were cool with how I'd changed. Still, I felt weird talking about it because I feared they might look at me differently if they knew the extent of my failures.

For the first year of being with Plus One, I carried the guilt and shame with me all the time. I was afraid that if I talked openly about my sin, it could potentially hurt the group. What if our fans found out I had failed in this area? I knew many of them wouldn't understand. I was also aware that many people would be hurt by my sin, and I just couldn't imagine sharing it openly. The risk was too great.

The Freedom of Forgiveness

I was carrying this weight on my shoulders when I met Pastor Tim that Halloween night. The night we prayed together in the front row of his church was the night I began to experience release from my guilt and shame. I surrendered everything. I gave everything I was. When, in my mind's eye I saw Christ hanging on the cross, I knew that He was hanging there for me for what I'd done. At that moment I began to realize the amazing power of God's grace. The reality of His love and forgiveness overwhelmed me, and that's why tears burst out of me like a flood. I had denied Him by my actions, and He still accepted me. For the first time, I accepted the fact that His sacrifice on the cross was enough—more than enough—to cleanse me from anything and everything I'd ever done wrong. I understood that His grace was sufficient for me (2 Corinthians 12:9).

That evening was the beginning of a long journey to freedom. Through memorizing Scripture with Pastor Tim, I've come to realize some very important truths. For instance, Romans 8:1: "Therefore, no condemnation now exists for those in Christ Jesus." When I read that Scripture, I could hear the voice of God telling me, "Jason, you are free."

For so long I'd been condemning myself for the things done in my past. Yet here was God telling me that I was no longer condemned for what I'd done. I no longer needed to live under a black cloud. Jesus had taken my condemnation upon Himself while hanging on the cross. Why would I want to grab it back again?

I also read 2 Corinthians 5:17, where the apostle Paul says, "Therefore if anyone is in Christ, there is a new creation; old things have passed away, and look, new things have come." As I read and memorized these truths, something wonderful began to happen: I began to believe them as truth. God made me brand-new in Christ Jesus. I am no longer the old Jason Perry who made such a mess of his life. I am a new person. I stopped listening to the devil and his accusations and began to allow the Bible to inform me about reality. God has declared me righteous in Christ Jesus. In God's eyes, I am now holy and pure.

This is God's grace in action, and I want everyone to know that God can set you free too. He knows everything we've done, but He's still willing to accept us and forgive us because of what Christ did on the cross. That doesn't mean that our choices don't have horrible consequences—they do. What it means is that the price for our sins has been paid. God no longer holds these things against us.

Because of Jesus Christ and the grace of God revealed through Him, I am now living a life of purity and hope. In a very real sense, I am a virgin once again. Jesus Christ has made me new. God set me free from every bit of guilt, and now I'm able to speak openly about Christ's power to cleanse us from sin. I no longer hide the fact that I've made mistakes; instead, I share openly about how God has forgiven me. These days, I receive hundreds of E-mails and letters from young people who are hungry to hear of Christ's forgiveness. Many of them can relate to the things I share, and I love to tell them that they, too, can experience the freedom that comes through Jesus Christ and His Word.

I want you to know that if you've fallen into sexual sin or any other form of rebellion, God will forgive you if you come to Him with a sincere heart. Don't let the devil drag you deeper, telling you that you can never be pure and righteous in the sight of God and man. Don't believe it. God will set you free from both the sin and its guilt. He has wonderful plans for your life, as He tells us in Jeremiah 29:11: "'For I know the plans that I have for you,' declares the LORD, 'plans for welfare and not for calamity to give you a future and a hope.'"

Identity: Singer

People often ask me when it was that I first began to sing. I tell them I started to sing before I could talk (at least that's what my mom tells me). I guess that means I've been singing for awhile.

Music was a natural part of my upbringing. When we kids would pile in the old station wagon with Mom and Dad and drive down the road, my family would get aggravated because I'd break out singing, making up songs about anything and everything. At first it was probably cute—then it drove everybody nuts. Sometimes I'd get in trouble for singing at school when I should've been quiet. It seems there's always been a song in my heart. No doubt, I got the itch to sing from my parents, who both have great voices and love to sing around the house.

My earliest memory of singing in public is that of performing at a third-grade talent show, where I sang a rap song that Carmen made popular. Several years passed, then one day my mom suggested that I sing a solo for church

CHAPTER SEVEN

one Sunday. I was about twelve years old, and I remember shaking so badly that I could barely hold on to the microphone. I was a wreck. It's hard to believe that I was ever that nervous, having sung on stage thousands of times since then. In those early years, I didn't sing in public very often, but it was just the beginning of this musical journey that God has allowed me to enjoy.

Seeds of Things to Come

When I was fourteen, my youth group traveled to a revival a few hours from my hometown. I'd heard about revivals before but really didn't know what to expect. All I knew was that sometimes God showed up in unusual ways.

We were there for three days, but it wasn't until the last night that God did something unusual in my life. It was a Friday evening, and the message was powerful. I remember praying fervently and crying out to God. I had never felt God at work in me like I felt Him that evening. He was doing something deep inside of me. I was so overwhelmed by God that my entire body began to shake. I was scared yet full of joy at the same time.

For the next three days, I felt God in a way I never had before. We arrived home on Saturday, and I was scheduled to sing for church on Sunday evening. I can remember being extremely nervous before getting on the platform, yet when I opened my mouth, I felt calm like never before. I could tell the Lord was moving while I was singing. People were touched. Some stood up and were clapping; others were crying in their seats. It was the most bizarre thing. I knew that it wasn't happening because I'd become such a great singer overnight. No, it was because God showed up. He was doing the work.

That evening at church was the beginning of something new in my life. From that point on, God put a desire in me to sing and minister for His glory. I had no doubt that God was calling me into a music ministry.

God confirmed my calling by giving me many opportunities to minister. I started singing regularly whenever the church doors were open—Sunday mornings, Sunday nights, and Wednesday evenings. People at church were so kind; they would always come up to me and say, "Jason, when are you going to sing again? We can't wait." It was humbling, yet exciting. God was using my gifts to minister to His people. It was a great feeling.

Building My Self-Esteem

As I entered high school, I became increasingly identified with my voice. I was leading my youth group in weekly praise and worship and singing by myself and with the choir each Sunday. When people thought of Jason Perry, they immediately thought of music, singing, and performing. I was the guy who was known for his voice.

And that's how I began to view myself. My life became wrapped up in my music to the point that I couldn't see myself through any other means. It became easy to hide behind the microphone. I enjoyed the gift and all the applause that came with it. Over time, I began to equate my walk with God purely in terms of how often and how well I was singing. My voice became the focal point of my life. It defined who I was. It became my identity.

I'm sure many of you can identify with what I'm saying. You have gifts and talents too. Maybe you're a good athlete or a good singer or you excel in playing an instrument in the band or the orchestra. Perhaps you are a whiz at computers or you are exceptionally smart and get straight A's in school. If you receive a lot of praise and attention for what you do, it's easy to let that particular gift define who you are. Anything can become a god—even good things that aren't bad in and of themselves.

That's what happened to me—I let singing become my god, my idol. I couldn't imagine life without singing. Whenever I'd get a cold and my voice would be gone for a few days, I'd become incredibly upset. I'd think to myself, *Jason, you'd be nothing if it weren't for your voice.* Obviously, I had built my self-esteem on the gift I'd been given and not on the Giver of that gift.

I struggled with this wrong sense of identity even through my first year with Plus One. I don't think I was aware of how much confidence I was placing in my own abilities. In my mind I had to prove to everybody that I could sing. It was important to me that I had the approval of every person in the audience, no matter where I was performing.

You'd think that I would've felt secure and successful. After all, I was singing all over the country with a popular Christian band. My dreams were coming true before my eyes. Yet all the record sales, the room service, and the tour buses left me empty and insecure. I was finding my identity in the wrong things. My focus was on me and my abilities, not on God.

Changing My Focus

As you've been reading this book, you've heard me talk many times about one of the most significant nights of my life: the night I prayed with Pastor Tim. That event was a milestone in my life, and it greatly affected this area of my identity as well.

When I gave my heart to the Lord that night, I gave Him everything. I gave Him my voice, my future, and my talents. It was difficult because I had put so much confidence in myself for so long. Yet God showed me that He loves me for who I am, not for what I do. He loves me because I am His child. Period. There's nothing I can do to make Him love me more than He does already.

Since that night, my focus has completely shifted from trying to please people to trying to please my heavenly

Father. I'm learning to look at myself through God's eyes, not the eyes of this world. I'm learning to relate to God as Jason, His child, not just Jason the singer. The difference is subtle, yet real. It means that now I'm more interested in the Giver of gifts than in the gifts themselves.

My whole world used to revolve around my voice. Now it revolves around God and becoming the man God desires me to be. I had grown up loving music, but something strange happened after I got right with God: Music became less important to me. In fact, I got to the point where I told God I didn't care if I ever sang again. For the first time, I gave my gift back to God. It was a little scary since I'd been holding on to it for so long. What if He took it and didn't give it back? But He didn't do that. In fact, I have more of a passion to sing for His glory now than ever before.

A New Identity

So what does my identity look like today? I can sum it up in one word: *freedom.* I am free. I used to be bound by the opinions of people around me; now I am focused on pleasing the One who created me—Jesus Christ. The apostle Paul experienced this kind of freedom and wrote about it in Galatians 1:10: "For am I now trying to win the favor of people, or God? Or am I striving to please people? If I were still trying to please people, I would not be a slave of Christ."

I used to spend much time worrying about small

things, such as, "Do people like my voice?" or "Do people think I'm good-looking?" I found myself trying to impress people for the wrong reasons.

There's nothing so freeing as learning to love yourself because God loves you. It means that you no longer try to be somebody you're not. I used to spend a lot of time comparing myself to others—maybe you do that too. Finding yourself in Christ is the only way to truly find your identity. Some people forsake God's path because they say they want to "find themselves." But how can people find their identity outside of the One who created them? It's a lie and it never works. It's just as Jesus said in Matthew 10:39: "Anyone finding his life will lose it, and anyone losing his life because of Me will find it."

Galatians 2:19b–20 also brings the point home: "I have been crucified with Christ; and I no longer live, but Christ lives in me. The life I now live in the flesh, I live by faith in the Son of God, who loved me and gave Himself for me."

My desire is that everyone who reads this book would experience the freedom to love himself. Believe me, I know it can be difficult. Everywhere we look, we see people who appear to have those things that we so obviously lack. In fact, many of us get angry at God, feeling that God has given gifts and advantages to other people while we remain lonely and slighted in the background.

I want you to know that God loves you just the way you are. He gave you your personality, your looks, your sense of humor, and your gifts and talents. When you downgrade yourself in comparison to others, you are denying the fact that God made you for a reason. Don't give in to this temptation. Instead, I encourage you to allow God's Word to shape you and form your identity. Surrender your life completely to Him, asking Him to mold you into His image. And do it on a daily basis—spend time thanking God for making you as you are for a purpose. Tell Him that even though you don't know what that purpose may be, you are willing to trust Him to reveal your calling in His perfect time.

The Bible's View of You

The Word of God has changed how I view myself. For instance, look at what Psalm 139:13–16 tells us about how God created each of us: "For You formed my inward parts; You wove me in my mother's womb. I will give thanks to You, for I am fearfully and wonderfully made; wonderful are Your works, and my soul knows it very well. My frame was not hidden from You, when I was made in secret, and skillfully wrought in the depths of the earth; Your eyes have seen my unformed substance. And in Your book were all written the days that were ordained for me, when as yet there was not one of them."

God had a strategic plan when He thought you up and put you together. It's not by happenstance or by evolution that you're here on earth. He didn't just throw you together as an afterthought; He carefully and meticulously made you. Therefore, if you spend all your time and effort trying to be someone you're not, you are robbing yourself of fulfilling His purpose in your life.

Don't rob yourself of the joy and fulfillment found in your unique identity.

The Power of Friendships

Why is it that nine out of ten testimonies include the following phrase: "I was doing fine in my walk with Christ until I started hanging out with the wrong people"?

Friendship is a powerful thing. Whether we have many friends or few, we were created for relationships. The people we call friends hold a tremendous amount of power over us. Since we are social creatures, those we spend the most time with heavily influence us—either for good or evil.

When I think of friends, my mind immediately goes to Josh, my best friend while growing up. Josh and I met in the seventh grade, and we continued as best friends all through high school. We did everything together. He played the piano and I played the drums, so every spare moment we had was spent at the church, banging on the instruments and having the time of our lives.

We loved to hang out overnight at each other's houses. One night Josh came over to play Monopoly, and we stayed

CHAPTER EIGHT

up late to finish the game. At 3:00 A.M. we finally decided to go to sleep, but instead told stories until our loud giggling woke up my mom. She marched in the room and began angrily addressing us. While she was yelling, I sat down on the couch and accidentally landed on a big bag of potato chips. *Crunch!* Josh keeled over in laughter, and soon Mom and I were laughing hysterically too. It's these kinds of fun memories that I think of when I think of friends.

Things were great between Josh and me until our junior year of high school. That's when I decided I'd rather be popular than obedient to God. I made some new friends, and they started to influence me for evil. Before long, Josh and I didn't have much in common. I felt bored when I was with him; I was looking for a thrill, and Josh wasn't into living on the edge.

Slowly Josh and I drifted apart. We no longer talked as often as before, and eventually we barely talked at all. He found out that I was starting to party, so he came and asked me what I was doing. I was so self-centered that I brushed him off, saying, "These people are my new friends, and if you really knew them, you'd like them too." I threw away a friendship that had taken years to build, trading a best friend who cared about me for friends who affirmed me only when I acted like an idiot at parties.

During that time of rebellion, I thought about Josh and remembered the innocent fun we'd shared together. I thought about the Monopoly games that lasted late into the night. Now to have fun, I had to do something crude, rough, or rebellious. I had to push the limits of what was acceptable and right.

When I finally came out of my rebellion, guess who was there waiting for me? You got it—Josh. Even though I'd pushed him away, he loved me enough to be there when I decided to get things right. He proved to be one of the best friends a guy could ever have.

Friendships are important because they often hold the power of spiritual life or spiritual death. I can remember a time when I wanted many friends. Now I have far fewer friends, but the friendships I have are truly significant.

Making Non-Christian Friends

What was it that caused me to hang out with those who were far from God? Actually, it started very simply. I started to spend time with a couple of non-Christian guys who didn't go to church and weren't serving God. We had some classes together, and it seemed natural to spend time doing things with them in a group. Though I was on the football team, I had never felt like a part of the "in" group. Hanging out with these new friends made me feel like I was getting there, even though I knew they were living a godless lifestyle.

As my friendships with these people deepened, I found myself doing things I never thought I'd do. I rationalized my behavior by saying to myself, "It's no big deal. Besides, my old friends need to get with the times." I no longer needed my Christian buddies—in fact, hanging around them became uncomfortable. Basically, I decided to cut ties with the people I needed most. At the time, however, I couldn't see how foolish I was.

My new friends introduced me to things I'd only heard about. I felt cool, and in some ways, I did become more popular. I was making a name for myself, finally getting more attention from everybody in the popular crowd. I was finally fitting in. So why was it making me feel empty?

Looking back on that season of life, it's obvious that the moment I shifted friends is when my life went haywire. When I lost connection with the friends who really cared for me as a person, I found myself drifting like a ship without an anchor. My values crumbled and my convictions softened. I traded the precious standards of my upbringing for the temporal pleasure of joining the "in" crowd.

Learning the Lessons of Friendship

From previous chapters in this book, you already know how my poor choices in friends affected my high school years. I wish I could go back and change some of those decisions, but I can't. No one can; once the decisions are made and acted on, it's history.

What kind of decisions are you making in your choice of friends? Let me encourage you to think clearly about the kind of friends you're making. The people you hang with says a lot about your walk with Christ. Are your best friends on fire for Jesus? That means you must be as well. Are your best friends lukewarm or worldly? If so, chances are you're not doing well in your walk with God. Your best friends can often act as a spiritual thermometer, showing the temperature of your spiritual passion. So let me ask again: Based on your best friends, what's your spiritual temperature?

Students do what their friends do. I was recently at a church where several groups of young people were in attendance. From the stage I could see a group of students who were into worship—it was obvious they were on fire for God. There was a second group of students sitting near the back of the crowd, not at all interested in what was taking place up front. I looked at both groups and thought to myself, *Wow, you really do become like those you surround yourself with.*

Let's say you hang out with students who come to youth group but run wild the rest of the week. Don't be surprised if you become that type of person. It may not happen right away, but it almost certainly will take place. You'll wake up one day and say, "What happened? I was so on fire for God. I was serving Him with my whole heart, and now look at me: I don't even want to go to church anymore. I can't stand the youth pastor or the youth group."

The devil enjoys taking people who love God and putting them with people who couldn't care less. For this reason, be careful whom you allow to influence your life. Keep in mind Proverbs 12:26: "The righteous is a guide to his neighbor, but the way of the wicked leads them astray."

The Positive Side of Friendships

So far I've focused on the impact of negative friendships. But let's look at the opposite scenario. Suppose you are a student who is passionate about serving Him. When even one person like you steps out and forgets about the popularity contest—forgets about trying to fit in and follow the crowd—it's amazing what can happen. If you have five or six good friends around you who are living with the same passion, you can become an unstoppable force. The unity and strength you draw from one another is unshakeable. What a difference you can make!

In high school I was a follower. I wanted to do what everybody else was doing. Now I'm seeing friendships differently. I want to be a leader and not a follower. I'm looking at friends and friendships in a whole new way. You might call them "friendships with a purpose." That means that there's a specific reason why I choose the friends I hang around with. The purpose? To grow together in Christ and to encourage each other in our walk with God. This doesn't mean that I don't hang out and have fun with my friends. I have more fun now than I ever had before. My friends and I will go out and have a great time. We love to be crazy and we love to laugh. But at the center of our relationship is a core vision that we all share. We challenge each other to stay sharp in our walk with Christ.

I don't want you to think that I'm encouraging anyone to form a clique. And I'm not suggesting that you act super-spiritual or that you only talk to your best friends. No way. The question here is one of influence. Be kind to everyone, but make sure that the "influencers" in your life are pulling you toward Christ, not away from Him.

When I think of students who made a difference at school, I think of Ricky Spindler. Ricky was in our youth group, and he was charged up for God. He was one of those guys who was always talking to someone about Jesus. At school Ricky was known for being a Christian, and even though he was sometimes a bit too loud or even obnoxious, he did his best to shine for Jesus.

For some of us in the youth group, Ricky was a little over the top. We would laugh and make fun of him for being so bold about his faith. I remember talking about him behind his back, saying that he was ruining people's perception of what it means to be a Christian. In reality, he made me ashamed because his brightness revealed my darkness.

Ricky's father wasn't around, and his mom was rarely at church, so he hung around the youth pastor quite a bit. Ricky wanted to change the world for Christ. Me? I just wanted to fit in and not make waves. I was the pastor's kid with a great family, yet I was the one who ended up tarnishing Christ's reputation, not Ricky.

I would give anything to go back and live my high school years over again. If so, I would be like Ricky. He didn't know it at the time, but I was watching him live for Christ, as were many other students. By witnessing, praying, and reading his Bible, he left a strong testimony at our school. Only God knows how many students were affected by his godly life.

Maybe you're not convinced that a few people who live for Christ can influence a whole school, but I know of twelve guys who, though pretty normal to look at, changed the whole world: the twelve disciples. They turned the world upside down because they were filled with the Spirit of God and were willing to sell out and be bold about their faith. I believe that you—along with several friends with one vision, one purpose, and one goal—could turn *your* school upside down for God.

Recently I was spending some time in prayer and felt God impressing something on my heart. I saw a map of our country, and on every part of the map, little fires were burning. They were small at first, scattered around the North, South, East, and West. Before long, though, the fires began to spread, and soon the whole map was ablaze. I believe that's a picture of what will happen in our country if students get serious about God. Even if only a handful of students at each school in our nation were sold-out completely to Jesus Christ, God could light a fire that would burn around the world. God can use you to light a fire for Christ right where you are. But you must choose your friends carefully if it's going to happen.

Accountability among Friends

If you've been around church for awhile, you've heard the word *accountability* used repeatedly. Just what does it mean to be accountable to someone? Ecclesiastes 4:9–12 says: "Two are better than one because they have a good return for their labor. For if either of them falls, the one will lift up his companion. But woe to the one who falls when there is not another to lift him up. Furthermore, if two lie down together they keep warm, but how can one be warm alone? And if one can overpower him who is alone, two can resist him. A cord of three strands is not quickly torn apart."

The Bible is clear that we need each other. No one can succeed in the Christian life alone—God created us to need other people. Sometimes I'll hear a person say, "It's just Jesus and me. I can have church in my living room if I want to because God and I can do it alone." That's one of the biggest deceptions the devil uses. Satan is delighted when we don't think we need other Christians in our lives because he knows that we become weak when out of fellowship with others. There is power in being with people who are like-minded. When you hang out with others who are passionate about God, you are adding a layer of protection to your spiritual walk. When you hang out with only lukewarm Christians or non-Christians, you are exposing yourself to the snare of the enemy.

So how does accountability work? What does it look like in a healthy friendship? Accountability takes place when friends help each other achieve what they really want to accomplish. Accountability equals change. Are your friendships resulting in your becoming more like Christ? The way to know if your friendships are spiritually healthy is to examine the fruit they produce in your life. For instance, do you and your friends waste a lot of time doing things that don't matter, or do you ever spend time reading the Word and in prayer? My friends are always asking me if I've been praying and reading my Bible. The core purpose of our friendship is to grow together into men and women of God.

A perfect example of what I'm trying to describe is found in the biblical story of David and Jonathan. Take a few minutes and read 1 Samuel 18:1-4. David had just defeated Goliath and was brought before King Saul. It was there that David met Jonathan, Saul's son. David was a shepherd from the fields near Bethlehem; Jonathan was the prince of Israel. Yet these guys became best friends; in fact, Jonathan's soul "was knit to the soul of David, and Jonathan loved him as himself." Jonathan loved David to the point that, after watching David defeat Goliath, he took off his royal robe and gave it to his friend. This signified that he was willing to let David be king, even though, as prince, Jonathan was next in line for the throne. That's true friendship.

New Friends and a New Direction

When I surrendered everything to the lordship of Jesus, I put every friendship I had under His control. It became apparent that some of my friends weren't serious about living for God, and I knew that I had to make some choices. Something had to give. If I wanted to walk with Jesus, I couldn't walk with some of the people I'd been hanging around. So I did some housecleaning. Without being mean, rude, or superspiritual, I consciously chose to focus on godly relationships rather than on relationships that would pull me away from God's best. Looking back, there is no comparing the life I now have to the life I had then. Poor relationships were robbing me of God's best.

You will pick your future by your pick of friends. Choose wisely and let God direct your friendships. Having many acquaintances can be a great thing—be friendly to everyone. When it comes to close friends, however, make sure that the people you hang out with are passionate about serving Jesus Christ. As it says in Proverbs 13:20, "He who walks with wise men will be wise, but the companion of fools will suffer harm."

Counting the Cost of Discipleship

Many students are familiar with what it means to be a Christian, yet they have never thought of themselves in terms of being a disciple. When most of us hear the term, we think of the twelve guys who followed Jesus from town to town while He was on earth. Yet Jesus says, "If anyone wants to come with Me, he must deny himself, take up his cross daily, and follow Me" (Luke 9:23). Discipleship is not something available only for a select few who lived a long time ago. It's also for us today.

So just what does it mean to be a disciple of Christ?

The word *disciple* means "to be a learner or a student." It also means "to follow." Before meeting Pastor Tim, I wasn't sure about what it meant to be a disciple. In some ways, it's the same as having a mentor; in other ways, it's more specific: Someone is discipled when he submits himself to another person for the purpose of learning how to follow Christ. Pastor Tim is doing just that: teaching me what it means to be a follower of Jesus Christ.

Jesus wants every one of His children to be sold-out disciples. Salvation is free, but it will cost you your life. True discipleship will cost a person everything. In Philippians 3:7, Paul talks about his extreme commitment to Christ, saying, "Everything that was a gain to me, I have considered to be a loss because of Christ."

What does all this mean? Why is Jesus telling us to take up our cross for His sake? The answer is simple, yet deeply profound. Jesus is telling us that we must die to ourselves and live unto Him. Instead of living life for our own interests, we are told to crucify the sinful desires that would naturally be in control of our lives. It's a whole new way of life—something that can only take place through the Holy Spirit of God.

The Spirit vs. the Flesh

You may not have realized it, but the moment you accepted Christ, you stepped onto a battlefield. You became not only a new creation in Christ Jesus but also a target for the enemy to attack. The Holy Spirit now lives inside of you, warring against the old nature (the flesh) that used to control you completely. That's why, even as Christians, we still have to fight the desire to do sinful things. God didn't remove our sinful nature; He just created a more powerful new nature inside of us. First John 4:4b says, "The One who is in you is greater than the one who is in the world." This means that we have the power to overcome sin. We must still choose, however, which one we want to control our lives: the Spirit or the flesh.

Jesus wants us to crucify our flesh by submitting to the Spirit. He knows that we can't overcome our old nature by ourselves, but only by the power God. A committed disciple is a person who is serious about living for Christ. We are saved by God's grace, which has nothing to do with what we can do for Him. But after we're saved, we are to live for Him completely; it's called taking up the cross and dying on a daily basis.

A Matter of Priorities

Why do some Christians stay immature while others become mature believers?

One thing I've noticed as I travel and meet people is that many believers have low expectations for the Christian life. Often believers see Christianity as an experience to add on to normal life rather than something that is at the core of their existence. Understandably, those who give little, receive little when it comes to spiritual fulfillment. I used to make excuses as to why I was not living totally for Christ. I'd say things like, "It's too hard to read the Bible or to spend time in prayer. It's not normal to witness or to live boldly for Christ in this society." I didn't put much effort into my walk with God, and I wasn't getting much out of it. My halfhearted Christianity was making me miserable.

Why is it that we are so tempted to live an uncommitted Christianity? What holds us back from enjoying God's best, causing us to take the road of least resistance? From my own experience, I've noticed a couple of things that hold us back.

Comfort. It's very easy to let comfort determine the choices we make in life. This applies not only to physical comfort but to emotional and social comfort as well. We've all heard people talk about the comfort zone: the state of mind that seeks freedom from difficulty or disappointment at any cost. Pursuit of the comfort zone can cause us to live idle lives, not taking advantage of every opportunity to make an impact for Christ. Living as a disciple, however, demands that we get out of our comfort zones. It's impossible to serve our flesh and serve Christ at the same time.

One day my roommate and I were driving home from out of town. The trip took about two hours, and we had a great time praying and reading our Bibles together the whole time. We were so fired up, we were preaching at each other. It was great.

When we arrived home, we were both so charged up that we felt we were going to burst. I looked at my friend and said, "Man, I've got to go and tell somebody about Jesus. I've got to tell people how Jesus changed my life."

"Where do you want to go?" he replied, ready for action.

"Let's go to the mall. No, better yet, let's go downtown." He agreed, so we jumped in the car and drove to the center of Nashville. We parked the car and started walking. It wasn't long until we came upon a girl who was sitting on the sidewalk, so we started sharing with her about the Lord. After a good conversation with her, we found several others who would talk with us about spiritual things. It was great. By the time we arrived home later that night, we were soaring on excitement.

God wants each of us to live life on the edge. Since that evening in downtown Nashville, I have been much more bold in my witness for Christ. I was scared to go, but when I stepped out in faith, God met me there. I have to admit I had been prideful about going downtown—Christian artists, for the most part, don't hang out with the homeless and needy. Yet God taught me some powerful lessons that day, and I long to be just as obedient in the future.

God is asking you to obey His voice. He wants you to step out of the crowd and be a leader, a disciple. Think about the joyful adventure that lies ahead. Instead of going to the mall to hang out, why not find ways to witness to people who need to hear about God? I don't want my life to be dictated by a fear of people's reactions. I want to make a difference. I want to change the world. I want to be so full of God's Spirit and His Word that I can't help but impact the lives of those around me for Christ.

Loneliness. Serving Christ is the most fulfilling and satisfying thing I have ever experienced, but sometimes I feel alone. I have no doubt that Christ is with me at all times; faith is trusting that no matter where I go, He is at my side. Yet with the people of His creation, being a leader sometimes means walking alone. Choosing to follow Christ as His disciple means that you've chosen a particular path, a path many of your friends may not be willing to travel. Being a disciple means you may find yourself dropping friends off at a theater instead of going in to see the movie with them. It may mean asking your friends to put on a different CD when you're in the car; it might even mean staying home on a Friday night because you no longer choose to join your friends in their activities. Disciples are different. They don't let loneliness determine their courses in life. Disciples choose their courses based on their Master's will, even when they go it alone. They remember that Jesus often traveled the lonely road.

A Matter of Obedience

Learning to obey God is at the very heart of discipleship. In fact, John 14:15 says, "If you love Me, you will keep My commandments." It can't get much clearer than that: If we don't obey God and His Word, then we have no right to say that we love Him.

Jim Elliot, a missionary who died for his faith in the jungles of Ecuador, said an amazing thing: "He is no fool who gives what he cannot keep in order to gain what he cannot lose."[*] That's counting the cost. If you live your life centered around gaining the world, then in the end you'll have nothing to show for it. Zero. Nada. Those who live for Christ, however, will make an eternal difference in the lives of people.

I hope you live for Christ. The life of a disciple is a life of sacrifices, but also a life of incredible joy and adventure. Don't waste your time on earth fulfilling the petty things of the flesh. Live for a higher purpose. And that higher purpose comes at the cost of things you may consider harmless—just as I considered my musical choices to be harmless, but they were turning me from God.

Discipled by Music

It was around age twelve that I started to listen to secular music. Until then I had only heard Christian music since we listened to a lot of Christian music around our house.

Around seventh grade, however, I started to listen to the radio on my own, branching out in my musical tastes. For

[*] From *Through Gates of Splendor* by Elisabeth Elliot

instance, from the moment I first heard Boyz II Men, I knew I wanted to sing like them. Their harmonies and their voices captivated me. I soon discovered a whole new musical world—Top 40 radio. My CD collection quickly changed; before, it was full of praise and worship—now, it wasn't nearly so uplifting.

I knew that the messages contained in the songs were not appropriate, but I rationalized my enjoying the songs by saying that I loved the sound and the beat but I didn't listen to the words. Yet over time, the secular messages began to change my attitudes and thoughts. It was very subtle; I don't think I was even aware of how the songs were affecting my mind. I tried to deny that my musical tastes were inappropriate, but deep down I knew the truth. Still, I wasn't ready to give up the tunes I enjoyed.

This battle continued to rage during most of my teenage years. Though there were several occasions when I smashed a number of my worst CDs, eventually I would go to the store and buy them again. Music had a grip on my life, and I couldn't shake it.

Music became my god, my idol. Whenever my mom would hear music she didn't approve of in the house, she'd tell me that it was changing my attitude. I didn't believe her, but I was ignorant about the power it had over me. Even when it began to affect my actions, I still couldn't see how I could ever give it up. Even now there are songs with disturbing lyrics that come to my mind, though I haven't heard them for years. This is the power that music can have; it can drag you down spiritually. Whether you know it or not, the lyrics will cement themselves in your mind.

My brother, Aaron, is two years older than I am. Some of our favorite memories center around working out together at the gym. He was always bigger and more cut than I was, and he never let me forget it. Still, we enjoyed our times together immensely.

To get motivated for our weight-lifting sessions, he and I would listen to alternative and rock music. We'd put on the music first thing as we entered the gym. As time progressed, I noticed a change in my brother. He started to become more angry than usual, often for no good reason. Outside of the gym, he began to show anger toward our parents and developed a short temper. The music was penetrating his mind; with their anti-Christian themes, bands like Nine Inch Nails and Tool were affecting my brother's behavior.

For a time, Aaron began to drift spiritually. His love for church and the things of God began to fade, and his desire for independence became all-important. He started going to various concerts and developed an addiction to the attitudes and feelings that the music created within him.

Since then Aaron has turned from listening to those bands. He came to realize that it was doing more than getting him fired up for lifting weights—it was changing his heart, mind, and attitude. It was eating away at his soul.

Cleaning Out the House of Entertainment

After praying with Pastor Tim, I began to look at my CD collection through different eyes. It was no longer acceptable to listen to music that was pulling me away from the purposes of God. This was a huge area in my life that I had to lay at the foot of the cross. It wasn't easy, but I knew I had to give it up.

I went through my collection and threw away anything that wasn't glorifying to God—one of the most freeing acts I've ever done. It's impossible to fill our minds with explicit or harmful lyrics, then expect to immediately switch over and worship God. It just doesn't happen. The Bible says that we cannot serve two masters. Jesus didn't say to His disciples, "Hey, follow Me—and, oh, bring all your CDs with you."

This was one of the areas where I had to give up some things for my walk with God. I'm so glad I did. Now, if I hear some of the songs from my old lifestyle, I'm amazed at the messages that used to run freely through my mind. God has changed my desires in this area; I now long to be filled with His Word rather than music that is blatantly against what the Bible teaches.

Am I saying that all secular music is wrong? No way. I am saying, however, that we must listen to music as if Jesus were sitting right next to us (which He is). If you don't think He'd be pleased to listen to it with you, then don't listen to it. Period.

The same goes for movies, TV, and other forms of entertainment. Even magazines. What's the point of encouraging worldly thoughts and desires in my mind? Why should I set myself up for a fall? Young people sometimes wonder why they fall into temptation without realizing that they often set themselves up for failure. It's simple—don't set yourself up for a fall.

The Father's Love

My father and I are very close. From an early age I have memories of his constant involvement in my life. Football games, Little League, concerts—you name it and he was always there for me.

I can remember fishing trips with Dad and my two brothers. Days in advance, we would get our poles and tackle ready, pack our food, and dream of catching the largest fish in the lake. The big day would arrive and we'd get up before the sun, pile into the car, and begin the long journey.

The road that led to the lake was full of hills; we boys called it the "bumpy road." My dad would drive fast just so we'd all get butterflies in our stomachs. It was a blast. Just imagine the scene: the sun shining brightly, the car windows down, and a father and his boys whooping and hollering in sheer delight as they speed along a country road.

CHAPTER TEN

For a kid, life can't get any better. I'll never forget the fun we shared on those trips.

Another great memory with Dad is the time he took me with him to Phoenix. Every year he'd travel to Arizona to attend a pastors conference, and each year he took one of us kids along with him. When my turn came, I was the most excited eleven-year-old boy in the world. It was my first plane trip, and I bugged the flight attendant for soda and peanuts during the whole four-hour trip. When we arrived at the airport and got to the rental car counter, Dad decided to get the coolest car they had—a convertible. Back home, the family car was a station wagon; for that week, however, we were riding in style. I was having the time of my life.

The highlight of the trip, however, wasn't in all the travel. It came on the last evening of the conference. The church where the meetings were held was next to a mountain, and it was a tradition that at least once during the week, each person in attendance would hike to the top of the peak. Dad and I waited until after the last service on the last night of the conference before we began our climb. After a long hike, we arrived safely at the top. The view was awesome. It felt as if we were on top of the world. The city of Phoenix twinkled like Christmas lights strung out at our feet.

After a few minutes spent gazing at the view, my dad sat down on a rock and called me over to sit with him. We began talking about God, our family, and the things in life that I was most thankful for. He asked me some questions about my walk with the Lord, then he began to tell me how thankful he was for me. He told me how much I meant to him and that he would love me no matter what I did or who I would become. I knew my father loved me, but when I heard it that night, I began to cry. Before long, we were both in tears, although with his big arm wrapped around me, squeezing me tight, I felt so safe—like I could stay there on that mountaintop forever. I knew my dad loved me for who I was, and his love made me feel secure.

I will never forget that night as long as I live. In fact, sometimes I wish I could go back to that moment. In my opinion, I have one of the best fathers in the world. I have so many great memories of doing things with my dad—playing basketball, going on trips, even ministering together. When I was fifteen years old, Dad was invited to preach in South Africa, and he asked me to go with him. We flew into Johannesburg and stayed there for three days before traveling to several other cities. We had a great time being together; we even got out into the bush and went on a safari.

I mention these events because they have to do with my earthly father. He's a good man, and I've been blessed to have a dad like him. I'm able to trust my dad because he's a man of his word. I know that he loves me not only because he says so but also because he shows me his love in many different ways. My point is this: If the love of an earthly father can be so great, imagine what kind of love the heavenly Father has for you and me.

God's Amazing Love

The Father has made us for Himself. The Bible says that we were created in His image, that we are His making (Ephesians 2:10). God has crafted each one of us with a special purpose in mind. He knows you intimately since He wove you together in your mother's womb (Psalm 139:13). He knows everything about you, yet He loves you with an unconditional love. You are precious to Him even if you have difficulty loving yourself.

God created humans for His own pleasure; we're made to worship Him. When Adam and Eve sinned, it resulted in humanity turning away from God and becoming separated from the Father. This separation meant that we had no means of getting back into fellowship with our Creator. We were totally helpless. We were lost with no ability to find our way home.

Then the Father did the unimaginable—something no earthly father would have ever done. He sent His Son to die on the cross for our sins. If you've heard this story a million times, then its impact may be lost on you. Pretend you're hearing this message for the first time. Pretty amazing, isn't it? Christ died so that you and I can inherit the love of the Father. Without this incredible love, none of us would have a chance to live with Him forever. Almost everyone has heard John 3:16, but listen again to what it says about the love of God: "For God loved the world in this way: He gave His only Son, so that everyone who believes in Him will not perish but have eternal life."

Another verse that talks of God's love is Ephesians 2:4–5a: "But God, who is abundant in mercy, because of His great love that He had for us, made us alive with the Messiah even though we were dead in trespasses."

In John 15:13 we're told that "no one has greater love than this, that someone would lay down his life for his friends." Through His Son, Jesus, God demonstrated this deep kind of love for us. Just as my dad showed his love for me in many ways, the cross is the primary means by which we know of God's love for humankind. We don't deserve it, and we certainly didn't earn it. It's a God thing. It's a part of our Father's character. God is love (1 John 4:16), and everything He does is consistent with His loving nature.

The Heart of the Matter

People have different views about religion—Christianity, in particular. Some see Christianity as a bunch of rules to follow; others think it's all about going to the right church or being born in America. But these things aren't at the heart of being a Christian. A true Christian is a person who has a relationship with the Father through His

Son, Jesus Christ. Jesus alone is the bridge to the Father—there is no other way to get to heaven. I've heard people talk about how they have some kind of connection with God outside of Jesus, but that's impossible; there is no way to have a loving relationship with God outside of a personal relationship with Jesus Christ. This begins when we completely surrender ourselves to His control and allow Him to be the Lord of life.

Maybe you're wondering how getting to know God works. What does it mean to know the Father and to become a part of the family of God? It helps to think of it in terms of an earthly family. When you were physically born into a family, you developed your identity from your parents. They named you and cared for you, and you garnered much of your self-worth from the way you were raised. This is similar to what happens with God's family. When people recognize their need to be saved from sin, they pray to God and ask Him for forgiveness. And because there is abundant forgiveness available from Christ's payment on the cross, God forgives them. At the very moment a person receives Christ, that person is "born again" spiritually (see Jesus' teaching on this in John 3). At that moment we become a new creation in Christ (2 Corinthians 5:17). God gives us His Holy Spirit to live inside us, and we are like a newborn baby in God's family. God is now our Father—the best father one could ever imagine.

Another picture of salvation is that of adoption. In Romans 8:15–16 we are told: "For you did not receive a spirit of slavery to fall back into fear, but you received the Spirit of adoption, by whom we cry out, 'Abba, Father!' The Spirit Himself testifies together with our spirit that we are God's children."

Adoption is a great analogy because it shows how God has handpicked us to be His children. I have a friend named Steve Keels who played a significant role in helping me write this book. Two of Steve's six children, Jason and Drew, are adopted. They're great boys, and like anyone who's been adopted, they sometimes wonder about their sense of belonging in their adopted family. A couple of years ago, when the boys were younger, Steve and the boys were lying on Jason's bed as they talked. He asked them, "Guys, does it ever bother you that you didn't come from Mommy's tummy like our other kids?"

Jason responded, "Yeah, I don't like it. I wanna come from Mommy's tummy."

Steve gently put his hand on Jason's little face, drawing it near to his own. He said, "Son, you are my boy. You are a Keels. You are mine, and you belong to this family as much as anyone else does." Steve hugged him close and wrapped him up in his fatherly arms.

Steve repeated this affirmation several times before he asked, "So, Jason, what do you think of that?" The little boy looked up and said, "OK, Daddy," then rolled over and went to sleep. He was secure in his father's love. He knew he was special in his daddy's eyes. From that moment on, he's had no more doubts—he knows he is a valued member of the Keels family.

If you've been born into God's family, then the same affirmation applies to you. You are His. No matter what you feel or what others may tell you, you are significant to the Father. You can enjoy the love of the Maker of the universe.

God Is a Great Father

I know that not everyone has had as wonderful an earthly father as I have. Some fathers are absent when they should be present, and some fathers are cruel and abusive. An E-mail I recently received drove this point home:

> My dad lost a big promotion at work; he ended up not only losing the job, but also getting a boss he couldn't stand to work for. So he started working at home and getting crabbier. Plus, we had to leave the house when he wanted to get high, so we were leaving literally all day so he could get high all day. The weekend after he lost the promotion was incredibly hard. I was very upset and frustrated. Friday was just a day where anything and everyone was getting on my nerves. By the time we got home, I was on the verge of

exploding (I'm sure you know the feeling). I sat down and got online and started to unwind. At the same time, I was making my dinner, because another thing about my family is we don't eat together—we make our own meals and eat whenever. So I was making my dinner and had stuff all over the counter, and it set my dad off. He started yelling about how there's never any counter space for him to make dinner and so on. Then he got mad that the trash hadn't been taken out. I so wanted to start screaming at him but I didn't; I just left the kitchen, ran into my room, got my Bible, and climbed on my bed. I was sitting on my bed and not thinking about anything, really, and I just started praying to God: "Dear God, hold me. Just hold me. Show me Your love right now. Be my father right now. Just hold me." I could literally feel His loving embrace envelop me. It's the greatest thing that's ever happened to me. For the first time in a long time, I felt loved and like I had a father right there, hugging me. I just kept asking God to hold me and I started crying. I haven't cried in a long time over something my father has done, but I felt like a little child in Daddy's arms again, and it was OK to cry. So I did.

Once a father has broken his child's heart, it's difficult for him to regain the child's trust. When someone in your life has walked out on you or told you that he doesn't love you anymore, the hurt is deep and real. Unfortunately, this can change your perception of what God the Father is like. Many people wonder if God can be fully trusted. They wonder if He's a good Father or if He is abusive, cruel, and selfish in the way He fathers His children.

Let me describe some ways in which God is a good Father:

God's fatherly love

- is not harmful;
- is not selfish;
- is not degrading;
- never leaves;
- is not like human love that is fallible and distorted;
- is unconditional;
- never cheats or is unfaithful;
- cannot be changed by anything you do.

I have been overwhelmed by the love of God several times in my life, but it was when I repented from my sin on that Wednesday evening with Pastor Tim that I saw for the first time how much God loved me. All of my sin and guilt faded away, and I began to understand that God's love wasn't dependent on how good or bad I was. Since that evening, I've been overcome by His love for me on many occasions. Sometimes while driving my car, I'll break down in tears, thinking about the undeserved love of the Father. It is overwhelming to me.

I am thankful for everything that God has given me: the opportunity to minister, the gift of music, the excitement of being with Plus One—all of it is great. Most of all, however, I am thankful for His unfailing love. It is deeper than I ever imagined and so wonderful that it will take an eternity to explore.

Prayer: The Relationship Strengthener

Every relationship requires a necessary ingredient: good communication.

The more I read God's Word, the more real He becomes to me. For years, though, I've wondered about prayer. I knew that I was supposed to talk to God, but to be honest, my prayer life felt more like a monologue than a conversation.

I decided to ask myself some questions, such as, "Who am I talking to?" and "Am I just blabbing or am I truly spending time relating to the Father?" These questions led me to search the Bible to learn more about prayer. I'm excited about what I've been learning.

For years I've wondered who I should talk to when I pray. The Bible tells us that the holy Trinity consists of three distinct persons who are equal in essence: God the Father, God the Son, and God the Holy Spirit. The Bible gives us many examples of prayer to the Father and to the Son, but rarely does it talk about praying to the Holy Spirit. For example, when the disciples asked Jesus how to pray, He taught them to pray to the Father (see the Lord's Prayer in Matthew 6:9–13). Jesus also said that when we pray, we should "go into [our] private room, shut [our] door, and pray to [our] Father" (Matthew 6:6).

Does this mean that we should never pray to Jesus? No, not at all. I pray to Jesus, too, but usually while thanking Him for what He did for me on the cross. I love to worship and praise all the members of the Trinity—after all, They are One. But it appears from the Bible that God the Father should be the focus of the majority of our prayers. It helps to know who you're talking to.

Also, I now treat God more like a Person than a genie. I'm embarrassed to think about the way I used to pray: babbling, rambling, no train of thought, not really knowing what I was saying. Now I pray as if I'm talking to a Person—which I am. I no longer pray just so I can say that I spent time in prayer. No, I really spend time talking with God. He isn't some inanimate force that gives me goose bumps and makes me feel good. He is a being who desires to talk with me on a regular basis. The more time I spend in His presence, the more I long to pour out my heart to Him. Prayer can be addictive.

Of course, good communication requires that both parties are free to talk. I've learned that God wants to talk to me, but if I'm always talking, I may not be able to hear His voice. There are times when we need to be quiet and listen—nothing more. God loves it when His children are attentive to His voice.

His voice can be heard in several ways, the most common being through His Word, the Bible. It's impossible to have a strong and healthy relationship with God without being consistent in reading and studying His Word. The Bible reveals God's will and His wisdom. If anyone thinks that God has advised him, yet the advice contradicts the Bible, you can be 100 percent positive that the Bible is the voice to be trusted over whatever the person thinks he's heard from God. God has spoken through His Word, and He will never contradict Himself.

God also speaks to us through other people, primarily believers. This happens to me all the time. I've noticed that when I'm praying about an issue or a decision in my life, God will often use wise Christians around me to give me His wisdom. They may not even realize that their words are an answer to my prayers.

In addition, God speaks to us by way of His "still, small voice." There are times when you know that God is speaking to your heart about a matter. It's not a loud or flashy message, but you know it's God, nonetheless. You can learn to recognize these moments of communication over time. It doesn't happen to me often, but when it does, I find that it's always in alignment with the principles of God's Word.

God is a wonderful Father. His love is available to anyone who will lay down sin and accept His forgiveness. No matter what kind of earthly father you've had, God promises to be your Father if you are willing to be His child and join His family. Don't let your family experience on earth hold you back from what God has to offer. If you've been hurt by your father here, trusting and loving a heavenly Father can be a stretch, yet it can be done. My pastor is a perfect example of overcoming the unloving example of a father. For some tragic reasons, he grew up never knowing his dad. To this day, he's never met his father. Yet my pastor is one of the best fathers I've ever seen. He has four wonderful children who adore him because he's raised them well. God filled the empty place in my pastor's life, and He can do the same for you.

God loves you; He really does. Get to know Him. Accept His love. Talk to Him often and read His Word. As you do, you'll find Him to be a Father beyond your wildest dreams, for now and all eternity.

Real Life with Plus One

"**W**hat's it like being a member of Plus One?"

I'm asked this question on a regular basis. Maybe the best way to answer it is to share some stories from life on the road. It still amazes me that God has given me these opportunities. I think every singer, while growing up, dreams of someday performing in stadiums full of fans who are screaming and going crazy. Amazingly, for this guy from a small town in Indiana, the dream came true.

Some Favorite Memories

I'll never forget the first professional basketball game at which we performed. Plus One had been together for about one year, and opportunities to sing were starting to come our way. One evening we were invited to sing the national anthem at the Staples Center in Los Angeles. Of course, this meant that we could see the Los Angeles Lakers from up close, which was another dream come true.

We arrived at the Staples Center early and walked through the underground passages toward the court. Everywhere we turned, we saw basketball players we recognized. We'd whisper among ourselves, "Hey, look. It's so and so." We were like kids in a candy store. We came out of the tunnels onto the brightly lit court and strolled to the middle where we did our sound check. As we finished, the Lakers came out for their warm-ups. There we were—on the court with Shaquille O'Neal and Kobe Bryant. Even Magic Johnson was sitting in the crowd. I thought I was dreaming.

Before long, the buzzer sounded and the announcer began his welcome over the sound system. Soon we were in the spotlight in front of eighteen thousand fans who were suddenly silent for our singing of the national anthem. The music track started and we began to sing. As the song progressed, my solo part kept getting closer and closer. I was so nervous, my stomach was doing flip-flops. As I stepped out to sing my solo, it was as if I was watching myself on TV. As I sang, I was thinking, *This is amazing. I can't believe this is happening.*

We finished the anthem and the crowd went crazy. It's a great memory, and the guys and I still talk about it to this day. Since that time, we've been privileged to sing at several more professional games, but I'll never forget that first one.

Another one of my favorite memories is of the time we were invited to take part in Michael W. Smith's praise and worship project. He was recording a live worship record and invited several artists to fly down to Lakeland, Florida, to be in the choir that would back him up. Plus One was invited to take part, but due to scheduling conflicts, only Nathan and I were able to make the trip.

We flew from Nashville with a number of other people involved in the project. When we arrived at the private airport in Florida, we walked inside and were greeted by such artists as Amy Grant, Chris Rice, and Erin O'Donnell. Everyone was hanging out and getting to know each other. It was fun because we usually do so much traveling that it's difficult to build relationships with other performers who also spend a lot of time on the road.

The whole experience was very laid-back. I had a great time getting to know people and spending time with the group in worship—those were my only responsibilities. The highlight of the day, however, was getting a peek into the life of Michael W. Smith. We did an interview together, and then I got to sit next to him at lunch. Michael has had so much success that I wondered what he would be like. As I spent time talking with him, though, I found him to be extremely down-to-earth. He was easy to talk with, and it was obvious that he wasn't trying to put himself above anyone else. He spent time with everyone who had come down for the recording.

I learned a lot from Michael W. Smith during that experience. Here's a guy who has touched the world with his music, yet remained a very real person. He went out of his way to make everyone feel comfortable and important. It reminded me of how people view artists as somehow different, but we're no different from you or anyone else. Besides the fact that we travel and make music, we deal with many of the same problems everyone faces. We want our fans to see that truth. Michael helped me to see that clearly.

Embarrassing Moments

Sometimes we are more human than we want to be. Embarrassing things happen that keep us humble, even during shows. For instance, during our first headlining tour in the spring of 2001, we had a show in Erie, Pennsylvania. Our venue for the evening was a unique, old theater. Just before the show began, we stood backstage, getting prepared to go on. The first number for the evening was called "My Life," a number that required a lot of energetic choreography.

Everything went well until the end of the song when we were to run around the stage, jumping like crazy. I ran from one end of the stage to the other, but as I neared the edge, I was blinded by some bright lights and ran full-steam off the edge of the stage. I landed on a big speaker case, right on my tailbone. The people in the first few rows didn't know whether to laugh or cry—their faces showed complete shock.

The fans may not have known how to react, but Nathan sure did. He stopped in the middle of the routine and ran over to see if I was OK, laughing his head off the whole time. Sheepishly, I crawled back onstage in time for the next number. Unfortunately, the choreography on the next song involved sitting down, and my backside was still sore from the fall. It was definitely one of the most embarrassing moments of my life.

Another embarrassing moment took place at a performance in Merriville, Indiana. We started the show in choir robes, singing the hymn "It Is Well with My Soul." After the hymn was over, the music track began blasting through the speakers and we were to rip off the robes and start doing our choreography. Unfortunately, I ripped off more than the robe. By accident, I grabbed my button-down shirt as well, pulling the shirt apart and baring my chest for all to see. Man, how embarrassing. Because of the choreography, I couldn't stop to button up my shirt. I had to keep going. So I buttoned as I danced, only to find out once the song was over that I had fastened the buttons in the wrong holes.

Wow, what a night. I was sure everybody had noticed what I'd done, but only a few people mentioned it after the show. Either everybody saw it and thought I was a fool, or they weren't watching me when it happened. Still, I can't remember being more embarrassed.

We laugh a lot when we go on tour because funny things happen all the time. Whether it's on stage or on the tour bus, the laughing is endless. For instance, one of our biggest jokes is the fact that Nathan will sometimes forget the words to songs. We give him a hard time, saying, "Come on, we've been singing this music for years." We always tease him about it.

And although life on the bus is a blast, sometimes it gets a little smelly. Five guys living together in small quarters isn't always a beautiful sight (what with Gabe's stinky shoes lying around). You get the picture. Still, there's never a dull moment when we're on the road.

Dealing with Attention

Perhaps the question we hear most often is this: "How do you deal with all the screaming girls?" That's a good question and is definitely worth an answer.

When I first got into Plus One, I was seventeen years old. I don't know of any seventeen-year-old guy who wouldn't enjoy having thousands of girls scream his name and hold up signs proclaiming how cute they think he is. What a life. Because I didn't have a strong foundation in the Word, this became a problem for me. I began to get caught up in all the attention. I had gone from being a normal high school kid to being a pop star in only a few months, and it went to my head. I enjoyed the fact that girls thought I was cute and liked my voice. When we talked with our fans, I saw it as a means of gaining attention rather than using it as a time of ministry.

After I surrendered my life to Christ, I immediately confessed this as sin. I knew that my focus needed to change and I needed to take the ministry I'd been given more seriously. Because my life had been so consumed with trying to impress others, God took me through a season where I began to withdraw from spending so much time with fans.

For instance, after shows we normally sign autographs and then hang around and talk with people. Instead, I would go straight to the bus and crawl in my bunk to read my Bible or call Pastor Tim. I needed some time to clean out the old ways of thinking and establish a new mind-set. If I had gone right back into the same situations of attention, I'm sure I would have fallen back into my previous ways. In a sense, God took me through a season of hiding. It took several months for God to clean me up internally before I could go back out and minister to our girl fans—I was determined not to be pulled back by the tricks of the enemy.

After several months of partial seclusion, I felt God releasing me to spend time with fans again after the shows. I got back into signing autographs and interacting with girls slowly, working to avoid a lustful mind-set. I didn't want to go back and flirt. I wanted it to be a time for ministry, so I asked the guys to keep me accountable. I set time limits for myself and let the guys know exactly where I was and how long I'd be gone.

Instead of seeing my time with girls as an opportunity for gaining attention, I now look at these girls as my sisters in Christ. It may sound a little funny, but it's the truth. I don't want to look at these girls in a way that would be impure or cause them to focus on me instead of on Jesus. Now when I look out at the audience during our concerts, I see world changers. I see godly girls who are serving Christ, and I don't want to do anything to discourage them from living for Him. My goal is that they would be drawn closer to Jesus Christ, not Jason Perry. I want them to fall head over heels in love with God.

A Message to Our Girl Fans

So how do I handle all the girls? First, I fear God, as well as the consequences of doing something stupid. Second, I focus on the fact that the girls who come to our concerts are our sisters in Christ. When I talk to our fans after the show, I don't want them to walk away thinking about whether I'm cute; I want them to know more about God. I refuse to be an object of false worship.

On several occasions I've needed to correct girls, telling them that they're behaving in an unwelcome way toward us. Does this mean that I don't enjoy having female fans? Absolutely not. It's great having girls for our fans, and I have a blast talking with them whenever we get a chance. God has allowed me to speak to the lives of many young people, and I am glad to keep even the slightest hint of evil out of our conversations.

Girls, instead of wanting to kiss and hug us, I'd prefer that you pray for us. Instead of giving us notes about our looks, why not write notes about what God is doing in your lives? I believe there can be a revolution if we seek God—a revolution of holiness, purity, and godliness. That's why I set boundaries in this important area of my life. I encourage others to set better boundaries too.

Once, when we had just finished an outdoor show in Florida, many of our fans were lined up along a fence to talk to us. At first I wasn't going to go out and sign autographs, but for some reason I changed my mind. I was walking up and down the fence, talking with people and taking pictures, when suddenly I noticed a young girl out of the corner of my eye. She must have been about fifteen years old and was wearing a shirt with a large Playboy bunny on the front.

I walked up to her and asked, "What's that on your shirt?"

She put her head down, then looked up and said, "I know, I know. I shouldn't be wearing this."

"Do you know what this represents?" I continued. "*Playboy* is filthy, and it totally degrades women." Her head was down again, and I could tell she was feeling convicted.

"I'll tell you what," I continued. "If I get you another shirt, will you put it over what you're wearing?"

Her face lit up in response. "Yes, please. Do you have a shirt I could put on?" I sent someone to grab a Plus One shirt from the merchandise table, and she put it on the moment I gave it to her.

All it took was her seeing that a young guy like me didn't think it was cool for her to wear a suggestive shirt. I want girls to know that it's unattractive when a girl dresses like she's interested in any guy at any time. When I see girls dressed this way, I not only turn my head away, but I pray for them. Obviously, there's a deeper issue—they are looking for affirmation in the wrong ways. My question is, Is that how you want guys to see you—as a sex object? Or would you rather have a guy know you and care for you because of your character, not just your outward beauty?

I love seeing girls who dress in a way that is not disrespectful to themselves. Girls, God tells us to be holy and pure with our bodies. Even though our culture tells you it's OK to wear clothing that is sexy or almost nonexistent, I want to challenge you to walk a different road. There are plenty of ways to be hip and trendy and to look great without being seductive or flirtatious.

But we are grateful for our female fans. And if girls are going to get attached to something, it might as well be guys who are serving God. The apostle Paul writes these words in 1 Corinthians 11:1: "Be imitators of me, as I also am of Christ." For us in Plus One, if that means signing a few autographs and taking a few pictures along the way, that's OK. As long as our fans are getting the message of what we're all about—encouraging people to live for Christ—we're headed in the right direction.

Dealing with Success

Another question that we hear frequently is this: "How do you maintain a level head considering all the success you're enjoying?"

I would answer this question by pointing to the rest of this book. Stay in God's Word, find a mentor, and build Christ-centered relationships to stay grounded. I hang around people who are honest with me. This is crucial because in my position I have people telling me what I want to hear and not always what I need to hear.

The biggest thing, of course, is keeping everything in the perspective of God's Word. In John 15:16, Jesus says, "You did not choose Me, but I chose you. I appointed you that you should go out and produce fruit." Ultimately, I know it wasn't up to me to be in Plus One—God chose to put me here. I know there are better singers and better-looking people in the world, but this is God's plan for my life. I'm so thankful for the platform He's given me.

I don't have any idea how long Plus One will be together, nor do I know what God has in store for me after He's done with this group. But I do know this: By God's grace, I intend to serve Him in purity, boldness, and with total abandon until the day I go to be with Him in heaven.

I'm counting the cost, and He is more than worthy of all I have to give.

Making
a Difference

After praying with Pastor Tim to recommit my life to Christ, I had an overwhelming desire to share what God was doing in my life. That next evening, Plus One went back on tour. After a few days, I got up the courage to talk about my recent change with a friend.

I said, "Hey, God really got a hold of me when we were home. He's really changed my heart."

My friend looked at me with a wry smile. "Really? Well, I guess we'll see how long that lasts," he responded. The sarcasm in his voice angered me.

I thought for sure this guy would be excited for me, but instead he shot me down. With one sentence, he took the wind right out of my sails. This first try at sharing what God had done in my life was less than positive, and I wasn't about to try again anytime soon. Apparently, not everyone was as excited as I was about my recent recommitment, so I decided to keep quiet. Besides, I wanted to prove to myself

CHAPTER TWELVE

that it wasn't just another two-week fling and to make sure that life wouldn't return to normal. Before I went shouting from the mountaintops, I had to know for myself that the changes were real.

Changes that Last

This book has been about change, about living a life sold-out for Christ. I have shared how God used His Word, people, and events to change my life in the hope that you will recognize God transforming your life in those ways as well. Yet why go through all of the effort and the sacrifice that real change requires? After all, you will still find trouble in your new life. If you're serious about living for Christ, you can bet on the fact that people will discourage you. They'll tell you that you're going through a phase or that you've "got religion." They might even make fun of you and tell you to stop trying to be so spiritual.

So why go for it with God? My answer is this: to make a difference. That's why I do what I do. I'm not comfortable being settled in my own relationship with God—I desire for millions of young people to walk in the freedom that I've experienced. In the position that God's given me, I want to do more than be a positive influence; I desire to truly impact people's lives for God.

Not long ago, we did a show in Alabama. The sun was setting as we got ready to take the stage, and I was anticipating that God would move in a great way through our concert. I'd been praying during the afternoon and felt that God was going to do something special. What it was, I had no idea.

The show began and we were having fun. There were a couple thousand people in attendance, and they, too, seemed to be enjoying themselves. As usual, we sang some worship songs in the middle of the set, then it was my turn to talk for a few minutes before the music started again. That night I shared my testimony. I felt free to share what was on my heart, and then we went back to the rest of the show.

As we finished up and came offstage, I was thinking about what I'd said. I began to feel insecure, doubting whether my talk was all it should have been. "Maybe I shared too much or it was a little too bold," I scolded myself. "After all, people didn't come here to hear me talk—they came to listen to Plus One sing."

We cleaned up and got ready to sign autographs. By the time we got to the merchandise table, hundreds of people were in line, waiting to talk with us. A lot of girls who came through the line were there for reasons other than wanting to encourage our walk with God. As I talked with people, I was listening to see if God had used my testimony, but hardly anybody mentioned it. I was beginning to feel like a failure—that what I had shared didn't make a difference.

We were almost finished signing when a young girl walked up to the table, holding something in her hand. She looked at me intently and said, "Thank you for talking about the cross tonight. The words you spoke changed my life." Then she gave me what she'd been holding in her hand—a cross.

I looked at this girl, not knowing what to say. A thousand people had just walked by saying things like "You're cute" or "You have a great voice." I was thinking that I hadn't done any good by what I'd shared. Only one girl came up and said she was impacted—and it was enough. Her story gave me hope that God had used me that night for His glory. If only one person was touched, that was OK—it felt wonderful to have made a difference in her life.

I want to make a difference. I don't want to be satisfied with having a career and making a little money—I want to truly impact the world. I believe I can and that you can too. God has called us to make a difference in the nations. We are told to go into all the world to share the good news of Jesus Christ. This is what makes life so exciting; I can make a difference in the life of someone, who then touches someone else, and so on and so on. We never know how our little link in the chain will influence eternity.

Plus One often receives E-mails from those who come to our concerts. It encourages us greatly to hear how God is using our music to help people in their walk with Him. Here are a couple of messages that came to us recently:

My cousin, or as everyone in my family liked to call him—my twin—was recently killed in a drunk-driving accident. He was leaving a party where the adult in the household served alcohol to him and his minor friends.

The reason I am telling you this is so you know that your music was and is an inspiration to me. Even through that rough time, your music showed me that God was still there for me. I say "still there" because even though I am only 20, I have screwed up plenty of times. When my cousin died, I was turning my back on God, but because of your music, I actually ran to Him.

I know you have probably heard this a million times, but I just wanted you to know that I admire you all greatly for being able to stand up and praise and worship God so freely.

Your music has helped me through a very tough time in my life. I recently lost my brother due to a heart attack. He died in March of this year. The day after he died, my mom bought me your CD *The Promise.* The songs are so beautiful, and the song "The Promise" especially helped me a lot. I know that, just like the song says, "God always sees your tears and hears your heart." Your music is so inspirational to listen to. Thank you for sharing your gift of music with the world. It has helped me a lot.

As Plus One, we don't take our ministry for granted. We are grateful to be in a position where we can influence people's lives. No matter if it's from a stage soaked in bright lights or from a seat in a high school cafeteria, you, too, can make a difference. Whoever you are and wherever you're from, God can use you in powerful ways.

Making a Difference with Nonbelievers

God is also to be praised when we get to be part of making a difference in the life of a nonbeliever. First Corinthians 3:7 says, "So then neither the one who plants nor the one who waters is anything, but only God who gives the growth." We need to be zealous for our faith and find opportunities to share Christ with our unsaved friends. Yet God is the one who causes the seed of the gospel to sprout in their lives, just as He did in yours and mine. We can preach all we want, but God is the only One who can bring life out of death. John 5:24 says: "I assure you: Anyone who hears My word and believes Him who sent Me has eternal life and will not come under judgment, but has passed from death to life."

You may then wonder, *Why bother sharing my faith with others? If God is in control of getting them to understand salvation, why say anything about the gospel? Won't they believe anyway?* Check out Romans 10:14: "But how can they call on Him in whom they have not believed? And how can they believe without hearing about Him? And how can they hear without a preacher?"

We must share the gospel with our friends. Nowhere in the Bible are we told to become a Christian and then just sit back and be happy. It says quite the opposite. God does the work, but He chooses to do it through Christians who are faithful.

The issue is not whether we should share our faith, but how to be most effective at sharing it. Let's say that you've recently made a commitment to live for God. You're now a born-again Christian—a totally different person than you were just a short time ago. How do you go back and witness to your old friends? After all, they may have seen you at your worst, doing things that were both stupid and sinful. They may even be expecting you to go out and be crazy with them again this weekend. How do you tell them that you've changed? What will convince them that you're different and that they can change their lives as well?

Start by living it out. When I was younger, I would get excited about living for Christ and would tell my friends that I was a changed person. Usually, though, this fervor didn't last more than two or three weeks. My friends grew used to hearing me talk about God, but they didn't see much change in my lifestyle to back up my claims. I was no different from everyone else. I may have talked about spiritual things, but my life was still similar to the lives of non-Christians.

Knowing What to Say

We've talked about loving people who are unsaved and sharing with them. But it's important that we know what to share with them. In other words, we need to have some answers. This is what it says in 1 Peter 3:15–16a: "But set apart the Messiah as Lord in your hearts, and always be ready to give a defense to anyone who asks you a reason for the hope that is in you. However, do this with gentleness and respect."

It's not enough to be a nice person—we must also be able to give some good reasons for why a person should believe the good news of Jesus Christ. This is big. Have you ever given much thought as to why you're saved? Or even what you're being saved from? If someone were to ask you why you're a Christian instead of a Buddhist or a Muslim, what would you say? These are the kinds of answers we must know if we're going to make a difference in this world. We must know what we believe.

After I first met Pastor Tim, we immediately began to study the Word of God together. We used a book on biblical foundations to guide us in our study. It starts all the way back with Adam and Eve and the original sin and works through the Scriptures to reveal God's solution for our sin problem: Jesus. The book explains ideas such as repentance, the lordship of Christ, and other basic truths found in the Bible. By going through the study together, Pastor Tim and I have explored many issues relating to our faith. It has helped me understand in detail just what happened when I accepted Christ and what it means to be a true follower of Him.

After going through the study, I am amazed at how little I knew from eighteen years of sitting in church. Before going through the book, I wouldn't have been able to lead a person to Christ by using verses from the Bible. Now I can, and it feels great. First Peter tells us to be prepared with answers, and that's what I'm doing: preparing myself for opportunities God brings my way. Before, I was afraid to witness because I didn't know what to say. I might talk about God and this cool feeling that only He can give, but I didn't know how to express the gospel in a way that would actually lead others to Christ. Now I love sharing the Word with people.

And when 1 Peter 3:15 tells us to have answers, that means people will be asking questions. Are you living your life in such a way that causes people to have questions about God? People notice our lives, whether we think so or not. They look at the way we respond to good times and bad.

Our lifestyle should be such that people wonder why we have so much joy. God is asking us to live a holy life according to the Bible and equipped by the indwelling Holy Spirit, and then be prepared when people have questions.

Jesus' approach was usually one of gentleness and outward love. Yes, He was harsh toward the religious leaders of His day, but only because their love of the law and tradition kept them from loving God and His people. To the common person, though, Jesus was open and kind. We should be gentle in our approach as well. Bold and zealous, yes, but tempered with a compassion that comes from being filled with the Spirit. As 1 Peter 3:16 says, we should share about our salvation with "gentleness and respect."

Walking through Open Doors

God asks us to live a life sold-out to Jesus by daily taking up our cross. He asks us to read the Word, pray, and obey His commands. As we live this way, we can trust Him to open doors for us to share our faith. When we tell the Lord that we want to witness to people, I believe that He is more than happy to give us those opportunities. He will bring people along our paths—people who are searching and ready to hear the truth.

It's amazing how God has been answering these types of prayers in my life. Even though I work in the Christian music industry, I have many opportunities to rub shoulders with non-Christians. It's so great to pray and then watch God open doors for me to share my faith. When I meet new people, I usually spend time asking questions and getting to know some things about them. Usually they will respond by asking me a question about what I do or what I think about current events. At that point, I'm in a position to share with them a few things about God and His grace. I never try to shove anything down someone's throat; neither do I try to dig unnecessarily into their personal life, analyzing their life story. I try to be bold and loving at the same time. If I sense that a person is open to discuss spiritual things, I'll do so willingly; if not, I don't push. I wait for the Holy Spirit to work, bringing people to a point of openness to God and His Word.

It's easy to act as if the world has the joy and fulfillment that all of us are seeking. The truth is, we Christians have what the world needs. We have the life-giving Word that can change people from the inside out. Yet for some reason, it's easy to be fearful about sharing our faith. We get scared, but we don't need to be. Second Timothy 1:7 says, "For God has not given us a spirit of fearfulness, but one of power, love, and sound judgment." There's no need to fear people if our focus is on the Father. After all, our aim is to please God, not the people around us.

At times I struggle with feeling unprepared to share the gospel. The devil wants to keep me quiet, so he'll whisper to my mind that I don't know enough about the Bible or that I'm too young to know what I'm talking about. The devil lies to us because he hates the gospel and wants to keep it from being shared with nonbelievers.

One of his greatest lies is that evangelism is best done by the professionals—pastors, ministers, and missionaries. If this were true, then the Church would grow at a snail's pace. The Bible says that pastors and those in professional ministry are to equip the body of Christ for the work of service (Ephesians 4:12). We are the ones who are to be trained and then sent out to do the work of ministry. Don't let the devil tell you that you don't know enough; if you know that Jesus is the Son of God and that He died for your sins, then you know enough to go and be a witness for Christ. By all means, get trained in the Word and in how to share your faith, but don't wait until you know everything before you open your mouth. Otherwise, you may never share your faith with those who need to hear about it.

I would never have written this book if I'd waited until I felt fully prepared. Yet I'm stepping out in faith and trusting God to work through me. Before starting this project, I didn't even care to read all that much, and now God has given me a book to write for His glory. Approximately eight or nine months before beginning this project, the Lord spoke to my heart about writing out my testimony and putting it into a book. I thought, *Lord, that's crazy. I don't even like to read. I can't write a book!* Yet God kept placing it on my heart and somehow turned it into a reality. Now the book is out, and I'm moving on to the next thing He has for me to do. God did it, but it took my stepping out in faith to join Him.

The same will be true for you. God will never give you a task for which He has not already prepared you. When He leads you to do something, it is usually a task that requires trust in His strength and not your own. So be bold. God has promised that His Holy Spirit is with us to strengthen us. There's no reason to fear.

Just before Jesus left this earth and ascended to the Father, He gave His disciples (including us) some very specific instructions. They are found in Matthew 28:18–20: "All authority has been given to Me in heaven and on earth. Go, therefore, and make disciples of all nations, baptizing them in the name of the Father and of the Son and of the Holy Spirit, teaching them to observe everything I have commanded you. And remember, I am with you always, to the end of the age."

This is what our lives should be about: going into the world, making disciples, baptizing them, and teaching them to observe His words. What makes this possible is what He says at the end of the above passage: "I am with you always, to the end of the age." I don't know when the end of the age will come, but I do know this: Jesus is with me always. He's given you and me these marching orders and the power to carry them out.

As I see it, this means several things for the young people of this generation. First, go into your school, your sports teams, your workplace, and your home and live a life that is sold-out for Jesus. Second, preach the gospel in love. Don't be intimidated by those who would discourage your efforts. And third, step out in faith and allow God to use you to make a difference in your particular sphere of influence.

God has called us to make a difference for Him. We were born for such a time as this. Let's not be counted with those who hold back out of fear or distraction; instead, let's take advantage of every opportunity to change our world for Christ. And let's start today!

Afterword

After reading this book, you may be thinking to yourself, *I agree with what Jason is saying, but I'm not sure how to make it real in my own life. What are some initial steps I should take to pursue God with my whole heart?* Let me encourage you to do several things right away.

First, tell a close friend about the changes you'd like to see in your walk with God. Be bold; don't hold back out of fear or embarrassment. Remember, true friends will want to hear what's on your heart and will encourage you to walk in the right direction.

Second, start to pray about finding a mentor. You may not have someone like Pastor Tim in your life right now, but I believe God will bring someone to mentor you if you ask Him and then wait patiently. He loves to see young people seeking godly wisdom from those who have something to share.

Third, get grounded in your faith by reading and studying the Word of God daily. The *TruthQuest Study Bible* is a great tool for students who are serious about learning God's Word in depth. I also recommend *TruthQuest Survival Guide for New Believers* by Steve Keels with Dan Vorm, a resource that will help you learn more about the awesome God whom we worship and serve, as well as many basics of the Christian life.

And if you get a chance, send me an E-mail and let me know how you're doing in your walk with Christ. I'd be encouraged to hear how God has used my story to draw you closer to Himself.

My E-mail address is:

jasonplusone@aol.com

and my Web site address is:

www.jasonperry.com

JASON PERRY

Also Available

The TruthQuest™ Inductive Student Bible (NLT)
   Black bonded leather with slide tab 1-55819-843-1
   Blue bonded leather with slide tab 1-55819-849-0
   Paperback with Expedition Bible Cover 1-55819-928-4
   Hardcover 1-55819-855-5
   Paperback 1-55819-848-2
   Expedition Bible Cover only 1-55819-929-2

The TruthQuest™ Share Jesus without Fear New Testament
(HCSB) 1-58640-013-4

The TruthQuest™ Prayer Journal
0-8054-3777-0

The TruthQuest™ Devotional Journal
0-8054-3800-9

TruthQuest™ Books
TruthQuest™ Survival Guide: The Quest Begins!
by Steve Keels with Dan Vorm
0-8054-2485-7

TruthQuest™ Living Loud: Defending Your Faith
by Norman Geisler and Joseph Holden
0-8054-2482-2

**Available at Your
Local Book Retailer**

BROADMAN
& HOLMAN
PUBLISHERS